Spinning & Dyeing the Natural Way

Spinning & Dyeing

the Natural Way

Ruth A. Castino

photographs by
Marjorie Pickens

VNR VAN NOSTRAND REINHOLD COMPANY
New York Cincinnati Toronto London Melbourne

To my parents, Nathan and Edith Agar

Cover photo shows the author's daughter, Robin Clements spinning flax into linen
with a hand spindle.

Van Nostrand Reinhold Company Regional Offices:
New York Cincinnati Chicago Millbrae Dallas
Van Nostrand Reinhold Company International Offices:
London Toronto Melbourne

Copyright © 1974 by Litton Educational Publishing, Inc.
Library of Congress Catalog Card Number 73-11758
ISBN 0-442-21482-0   cloth
      0-442-21483-9   paper

Designed by Morris Karol

Published by Van Nostrand Reinhold Company
A Division of Litton Educational Publishing
450 West 33rd Street, New York, N.Y. 10001

16 15 14 13 12 11 10 9 8 7 6 5 4 3

Library of Congress Cataloging in Publication Data

Castino, Ruth, 1929–
  Spinning and dyeing the natural way.

  SUMMARY: Includes information about spinning with
spindles and spinning wheels, yarn preparation, dyeing
with plants, various fibers, and weaving.
  Bibliography: p.
  1. Hand spinning. 2. Dyes and dyeing, Domestic. [1. Hand spinning. 2.
Dyes and dyeing] I. Pickens, Marjorie, 1931– illus. II. Title.
TT847.C37 746.1'2 73-11758
ISBN 0-442-21482-0

Contents

Acknowledgments

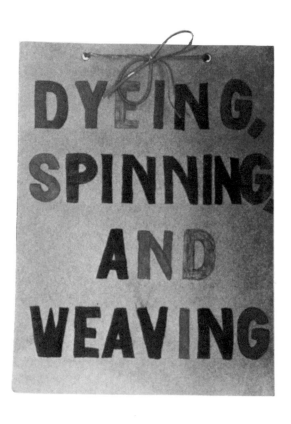

I would like to express my gratitude to the Wool Education Center, Denver, Colorado, for the facts and pamphlets they supplied me regarding wool production, and to the National Cotton Council of America for their informative booklets.

My thanks to Mr. Thomas Olsen, principal of Brookside Elementary School, Westwood, New Jersey, for his enthusiastic cooperation and interest; to fifth-grade teachers Miss Nancy Brown and Mrs. Joan Waneck for their aid, cooperation, fortitude, patience, and good nature through the more hectic days; to the Brookside Home School organization for their foresight and initiative in making spinning and dyeing a part of the school curriculum; and a special thanks to the boys and girls of Miss Brown's and Mrs. Waneck's classes, who worked so hard and so well to make this book a reality.

My appreciation goes also to Brownie Troop 14, Junior Troop 234, and their leaders, Mrs. Evelyn Haight, Mrs. Rita Di Matteo, and Mrs. Diana Wood, all of Sloatsburg, New York, for tramping through woods and fields with us; to my former apprentice Becky Miller, whom I could always count on; to the administrators and my students at Newark College of Fine and Industrial Arts, and finally, to photographer Marjorie Pickens for her many hours of lens snapping and darkroom work, which provided all the excellent photographs for our book.   R.C.

An Open Letter from the Spinster

How a city-bred girl like me ever wound up behind a spinning wheel is a question to be answered only in the writing of yet another book. Suffice it to say I have found my true vocation as a "spinster" and a form of happiness and serenity that I can only be grateful for. Before my husband and children take offense, let me explain that a spinster is the feminine term for one who spins; a spinner is a man who spins. Its connotation of "old maid" perhaps derives from the fact that the eldest unmarried daughter was often left the task of spinning the family's supply of yarn in the old days.

As a textile craftsman seeking a more original approach to the designing of creative stitcheries, I turned to the age-old craft of spinning fibers into yarn. Thus new vistas unfolded before me, and I learned a way of life which brought me quite literally back to nature. For, while acquiring fibers to spin, I became the proud owner of a small flock of sheep and a family of angora rabbits. My dyepot experiments have led me through many woods and across countless fields, and I have learned not only to respect "weeds" but to admire and seek out these plants, which actually deserve the name of wild flowers.

In my work with young people from preschool to third year college level, I find an eagerness to absorb knowledge of the basic structure of the yarns and threads that eventually create fabrics. "Awe-struck" is the best word to describe their attitude when they lift a yellow mass of fleece from a pot filled only with water and cooked goldenrod.

This craft has brought me much pleasure, many adventures, new friends, great satisfaction, and some chuckles, especially when I have overheard common misconceptions about spinning and dyeing as I demonstrated the crafts. Cotton does *not* grow on sheep, I don't *skin* cats to spin their fur, I don't boil *bugs* for color, and goats and sheep are two entirely different animals! I hope this book dispels these rumors, and provides many readers with a new, satisfying way of life. Happy spinning!   R. C.

1 Plants + Sheep = Yarn

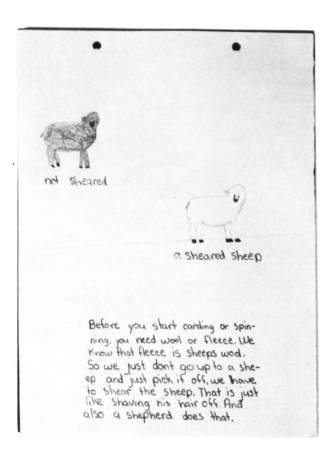

not sheared

a sheared sheep

Before you start carding or spinning, you need wool or fleece. We know that fleece is sheeps wool. So we just dont go up to a sheep and just pick it off, we have to shear the sheep. That is just like shaving his hair off. And also a shepherd does that.

How It All Began

When asked to demonstrate handspinning and nature dyeing in elementary schools, I invariably begin my program with the story of Moe, the lazy caveman. Because archeologists have unearthed the remains of spindle whorls at the site of Stone Age caves, we can only surmise that it was in this prehistoric era that man first spun. The whorl, together with a shaft, forms the hand spindle, the simplest tool for spinning fiber into yarn. In prehistoric days the whorl was made of stone, although now the whole spindle is usually of wood.

I tell the youngsters that possibly because Moe was too lazy to sharpen his spears, he became quite nervous one day when told by neighbors that a ferocious saber-toothed tiger was heading his way. Pacing his cave, wringing his hands in despair, he unwittingly plucked some hairs from an animal companion. In his agitation he began to twist these fibers between his fingers, expecting to meet his doom any moment.

My story has a happy ending, however, for by and by the neighbors informed Moe that the tiger had changed course, and Moe was safe. He learned two valuable lessons that day: never let the spear points get dull, and hairs twisted between one's fingers make a long, continuous, rather strong strand of stuff.

Today we refer to this "stuff" as yarn or thread, and to Moe's hairy companion as a sheep. In all likelihood, sheep were around in his day, too. They were domesticated from wild species, such as those that now exist in Europe and Asia, during the Neolithic times. From these small, hairy animals of prehistory, many specific breeds have been developed through the ages, some noted for their meat (English Wiltshire Horn), some for milk and cheese (East Friesian of Germany), while others are raised especially for the soft mass of fleece which envelops them (Merino).

Grease fleece right after shearing, composed of many "locks."

Wool as a Fiber

Although I handle many fibers, both animal and vegetable, I spin and dye more wool than any other. Because of its many fine qualities, this product of the sheep has been a favorite of man for centuries. As early as the days of the cave man, it was discovered that wool gave great protection from the elements. We know now that the fiber's ability to entrap air particles makes wool fabrics ideal insulators. In cold climates, they keep out the chill and hold in the body heat. In warmer climates, they allow air circulation and evaporation of perspiration. Sheep have played an important part in many countries' histories. Sheep were not native to North America, and first arrived on the ships of the Spanish conquistadors.

Although during American Colonial days, much fine woolen cloth was still imported from England, to encourage production in the Colonies, laws were passed requiring each family to spin and weave homespun cloth. George Washington bred a fine flock of sheep at his Mount Vernon home, and the suit for his presidential inauguration was wool.

There are many different breeds of sheep with wool of varying types. Merino, for example, originating in Spain and Rambouilet, originating in France, both produce very fine-textured wool; Hampshire, a British breed, has medium wool; Romney, also originating in Britain, has long wool; and from the Caspian region comes the Karakul, whose fleece is used for spinning in the United States and other countries but whose tightly curled lamb's wool is used as a pelt in the Middle East and European countries. The Navajo Indians of the American Southwest, famed as weavers, when they spun yarn instead of unravelling it from trade blankets, traditionally used the fleece of a small, slender, hardy sheep considered to be remnants of Spanish Churra sheep brought by early settlers. Each breed's wool has characteristics of its own, and the spinner or dyer chooses a specific fleece to adapt to his techniques or to suit the use to which he intends to put the finished yarn.

A fleece is comprised of many "locks," or clumps of fiber, some silky and soft, some coarse and dry. At least four types of wool fiber can be found in one fleece, as well as hay, burrs, dead bugs, seeds, manure, dried mud, lanolin, and sheep sweat (suint). These last two combine to produce a greasy coating sometimes called "yolk." Although spinning can be done from a "grease fleece," and in fact may be easier for a beginner, it is difficult to judge the size of the yarn produced, because the fibers will fluff up after washing.

Thus, before we begin to spin our fleece into usable wool yarn, it is necessary to:
1) separate it from the sheep (shearing)
2) sort it by hand
3) clean it (picking, teasing, and washing)

9

The Fleece

Mr. Gerrit Zwolle is a sheep shearer. Though he follows an odd occupation for the New York Metropolitan area, he manages to shear some 1,500 sheep a year. When I invited him to visit a class of ten-to-eleven-year olds, he brought along a young Hampshire ewe, who soon enough presented us with a soft fleece. Luckily it was a nice enough day for the sheep shearing to take place outside. All the shearer needed was a long extension cord for his electric shears. This job, though, can as well be done in a classroom, auditorium, or gymnasium.

Shearing is a skilled occupation, and a good shearer can separate the entire fleece from the sheep in one piece. If areas of wool remain, a second cut must be made. Although this can be spun too, it is less desirable because the fibers are necessarily shorter than those from the first cut.

Sheep, by the way, make rather sweet pets. One of the easiest animals to care for, they provide companionship, trim the grass, supply fertilizer, and "give of their fleece to spin up." Raising a lamb or two would be an interesting home or school project, and save on lawn maintenance!

Gerrit Zwolle, sheep shearer, and young Hampshire ewe.

Sheep shearing with an electric shears. Fleece should come off entirely in one cut.

After shearing, the sheep's natural white color shows clearly, although the dirty fleece appears darker.

SORTING

The best fleece is found in the "extra diamond," or shoulder and flanks of the animal. This is of good length and luster, with a nice "crimp," or wave, to it. The rear quarters of the sheep produce a coarser fiber "britch" and "prime," often used in rug production. Some of this contains tags of manure which make excellent garden fertilizer. The "diamond" section of the fleece lies along the ridge of the back. This generally produces a nice yarn if it has not been overexposed to the elements. Fleece locks from the head, "shafty," are on the short side but of nice quality.

Sorting, then, is a simple hand operation necessary to separate fleece found in these four areas on the sheep — shoulder and flanks, rear quarters, ridge of the back, head — as well as fleece of different crimp, color, or texture found within each of the four or more sorted piles. Some of the fleece may be quite yellow where lanolin has accumulated, and some may be dry, oily, dull, or lustrous in texture.

Picking usually goes along with sorting. The wool is separated or loosened so that any seeds, hay, other plant matter, or lumps of dirt will fall out. Often this is done by holding a large clump of fleece in one hand, and rapidly plucking it to eliminate all clumps with the other. The result is a soft, fluffy mass. I sometimes enjoy spinning an unpicked but relatively clean fleece, and seeing the little seeds fly out from the spinning wheel in an altogether natural way.

For the nicest yarn, use one type of fleece lock rather than mix them.

Sorting fleece into different quality fibers while removing hay, burrs, and other foreign matter.

Teasing the locks, like "teasing" hair, fluffs it up. It also further cleans it.

Teasing, or "picking" as it is sometimes called, is done by holding a small clump lightly with the fingers of one hand and plucking at it with the other, thus breaking up the individual locks.

WASHING

As mentioned, the mass of fiber sheared from the sheep has an oily content. If spun without washing, the resulting grease yarn will make water-resistant cloth, like that in fishermen's sweaters. If the sheep has been properly cared for, there is no unpleasant odor to this yarn. To the contrary, it has a sweet aroma.

Washing, to remove the mixed lanolin and suint, is best done on a well-picked fleece. That way, fibers are free of extraneous matter and the fleece is fluffed up to ensure quicker penetration of water and soap. Very hot water from the tap, and enough soap to make a nice froth, will soon make a drab-looking fleece appear sparkling white. Be careful while washing not to agitate the fibers too much. Rinse in hot water, as wool should not be subjected to harsh changes in water temperature, which can cause matting. In rinsing, squeeze, do not twist the fibers.

Washing the fleece gently in hot water and liquid soap to remove the lanolin and sheep sweat.

Hot water must be used for rinsing, as changing water temperature may mat the fleece.

Once washed, the fleece is collected and hung to dry. Convenient tree branches, not in full sun, are fine drying racks. Fences or other racks indoors, where air can circulate, are also good. If you are going to dye the wool, do not dry it at this point. Instead, begin the dyeing procedure right after washing, as the wool must be wet for any chemical substance to penetrate. Grease yarn cannot be dyed at all, because the oil prevents penetration of the dyes. From a spinster's point of view, it is best to wash and dye wool in the fleece, although it can also be done after spinning, in the skein.

Materials needed for washing are:

    1 large sheep fleece (this will serve about 60 people, allowing each about two handsful of fleece)
    liquid soap
    2 laundry tubs (or a double sink)
    1 drying rack, fence, or large tree

Drying fleece on a convenient tree.

14

Dyeing the Fleece

After shearing, sorting, picking, and washing the fleece, the next process is dyeing. Many natural and synthetic pigments are able to impart color to fleece, but those that come from natural plant sources are the most subtle and varied. Colors can be obtained from dyeplants that grow all about us, in fields, woods, on mountainsides, in marshy areas, deserts, empty lots, and even sidewalk cracks. The study of dye plants and the colors they produce has fascinated men of all ages and lands. In fact, special techniques for obtaining certain hues have at times been carefully guarded as precious secrets.

Wher. man first began to put color into fibers, he found it would not remain, but would fade in sunlight and run when wet. Something had to be done to the fiber before it went into the dyebath, in order to fix the color. The various substances that are added to the wool before it is dyed are called mordants or fixatives, and some of them are as common as salt or vinegar. In early America, noting that rust stains remained fixed in their fabrics, the women mordanted wool with rusty nails before dyeing.

The fascination of nature or vegetable dyeing is in the endless varieties of colors and shades provided to the dyer by Mother Nature. One plant will yield more than one color, depending on the mordant used in combination with it. For example, goldenrod will give a sun-bright yellow on an alum/cream of tartar mordanted fleece, a grand rust orange when chrome salts are used, and shades of green with iron salts.

Chapter 2 will give some recipes and all you need to know to begin your own experiments in mordanting and dyeing. After reading it, you may want to pursue the subject with the aid of some excellent books on nature dyeing listed in the Bibliography.

No, they are not cooking spaghetti! They are mordanting already spun yarn in preparation for dyeing.

15

Field Guide to Common Dyeplants

Field guide identifications are given on pages 16–19. Instructions for mordanting and dyeing with plants may be found in Chapter 2, together with a list of these and other plants from field, garden, and kitchen, giving common and botanical names, and dye colors with various mordants.

Shown opposite

1. Black-Eyed Susan. Grows in fields and along roadsides. Pick the above-ground plant during the summer when it flowers.
2. Chrysanthemum. A cultivated garden flower. Pick flower heads when they bloom in late summer and fall.
3. Common Evening Primrose. Grows in fields, vacant lots, and along roadsides, usually in full sun. Pick the above-ground plant in summer, when it flowers, about three-quarters of the way from the ground level, to avoid too much stalky material.
4. Coreopsis. Grows wild or in gardens. Pick flowers when they bloom in summer.
5. Dahlia. A cultivated garden plant. Use flower heads, especially the red ones, when blooming in mid-summer.
6. Dandelion. A very common weed of lawns and fields. Use above-ground plant, or flowers alone, which give paler shades. Blooms in spring and summer.
7. Daylily. Garden plant, but also grows along highways and in light underbrush. Pick flowers when they bloom in late spring and early summer.
8. False Solomon's Seal. A wild flowering plant of shady woods. Pick berries, which are ripe in the autumn. This is a rare plant, however, and should be used only sparingly. See remarks on page 33.
9. Goldenrod (right); Dock (left). Goldenrod is one of the most common weeds, and can be found even in tiny patches of grass growing in the cracks in city sidewalks. Use the above-ground plant when it flowers in August and September.

   Dock is a pest in the garden, with deep roots. Grows well along roadsides and in vacant lots. Pick the autumn-browned tops of the plants.
10. Iris. A cultivated garden plant. Pick the purple petals in early summer when they flower.

Field guide captions continue on page 19.

1

2

3

4

5

6

7

8

9

10

11. Jewelweed. North America. Grows in lightly wooded, moist areas, and along streams and ditches. Pick above-ground plant when it flowers in summer.

12. Maple-Leaf Viburnum. Grows on the sunny edge of woods in among maple and oak trees where woods are not dense. Pick the ripe berries in autumn.

13. Marigold. A common garden plant. Use flowers, which bloom all summer long.

14. Mullein. Grows in fields, lots, along roads, on sunny slopes. Pick the above-ground plant in autumn and even after frost. This dyeplant dries well.

15. Mustard. Grows as a weed in cultivated fields and wastelands. Pick above-ground plant when it flowers in spring.

16. Pokeweed. North America. A common weed of lots and fields, even in cities. Pick the berries when they are ripe in late summer.

17. Queen Anne's Lace. One of the most familiar wild flowers, which grows in fields, and an occasional back-yard, as a weed. Pick the above-ground plant in early summer, when it is young and tender.

18. Ragweed. Grows in fields and vacant lots, along high-ways and at edge of woods. Pick the above-ground plant in summer, before the tiny buds open. Ragweed causes hayfever in people allergic to its pollen.

19. St. John's Wort. Grows well in full sunshine in fields, lots, roadsides, and rocky areas. Pick the above-ground plant when it flowers from spring through autumn.

20. Staghorn Sumac. A common shrubby tree of lightly wooded areas. Pick leaves and stems in late summer and early autumn. Dry them before using, for best results. Make sure you know the sumacs before picking them — the white berried sumacs can cause a poison-ivy like rash. Pick only red-berried sumacs, such as the staghorn.

2 Using Plants to Dye With

Nature dyeing is an ancient craft, and the plant-mordant recipes are many and varied, having been accumulated over centuries in traditional lore. Perhaps it seems confusing to deal with chemicals and weeds and simmering dyebaths in order to color wool, but the processes are really no more difficult than cooking, and the transformations are magical.

As a dyer, you must learn to pay attention to Mother Nature before she will yield her secrets. Not only must you learn to identify the plants mentioned in this and other dye books, but you must learn to gather them at the right time of year — many flowers and leaves in spring or summer, berries in autumn. The same plant material taken at different seasons may produce different colors, and some may produce no dye at all at the wrong time of year. The illustrated field guide and its list on page 16 will help you find plants mentioned in this book, and at the right time. Many are common roadside or field weeds throughout the country, and some even grow in urban areas. If you are going to go further in dyeing, learn to know plants well. A good field guide, such as those listed in the Bibliography, is essential.

Next, you must learn what to expect from plants in the dyepot. Some produce their own colors or similar shades, like the dark pink from purplish black elderberries, and others are more surprising. All dahlias produce a yellow dye, no matter what the color of the flowers. In fact, the red dahlias give the strongest yellow. A list of plants and the colors they yield, alone or with mordants, can be found on pages 33, 34, and 37.

You must learn to pay attention to Mother Nature before she will yield her secrets. The student is examining thistle seed hairs, which, like milkweed and cattail seed hairs, can be spun up with wool. He is collecting sumac and ragweed for dyeing — red-berried sumacs are harmless, but white-berried sumacs can cause a severe rash. Ragweed causes hayfever in some people.

Gathering and Preparing Plants for Dyeing

As dye plants grow all about us, a field trip to gather them may not have to range very far from home or school. Any picnic or outing can be an excuse to look for them. Even if such trips are infrequent, as in a class field trip, enough material can be gathered to last the whole winter. In cold climates, when winter stills the growth of plants, make use of the plants picked on summer field trips and then stored, or turn to your own kitchens for such materials as carrot tops, onion skins, spinach, and the juices of fresh, frozen, or canned vegetables and fruits.

Consider Nature's balance and the preservation of natural beauty when gathering plants. Leave enough of each plant standing so that it can naturally reseed itself (that is, unless you're picking dandelions from your own lawn!), and never pull up roots haphazardly. Be sure that in taking bark from trees, you gather only from downed branches or, very sparingly, from twigs. If the bark of any tree is cut in a complete circle around the trunk ("ringed") the tree will die because the flow of nutrients from the roots has been interrupted. Check before going on a field trip about which plants are forbidden or inadvisable to pick in your area — they may seem like weeds to you but still be rare, or even poisonous. The various conservation, park and recreation, fish and wildlife, or agriculture departments, as well as a local botanical garden, may be able to advise you. Do not pick any plant material at all within public lands or parks unless you have permission.

Once picked, the plants must be sorted. Plants with

A short field trip can produce enough dyeplant material to last you through the winter.

Dyeplants grow all around us. This student has found some common evening primrose. When picking plants, always leave enough growing so that they can reseed themselves. Don't pull up anything by the roots, unless you are specifically gathering roots.

Gathering the *inner* bark of the white birch tree. Always use fallen boughs, not only because they yield the best dye but to aid in preserving living trees. Never ring the bark of any tree, that is, cut it in a full circle. The tree will die because nutrients cannot flow up from the roots.

long stalks, such as goldenrod, sumac (pick only the red-berried sumacs, the white-berried ones cause a severe rash) and jewelweed and ragweed (North America) are easily handled when tied in bunches and wrapped around the stalks with cord or rubber bands. Berries can be stored in closed jars. Many dyers prefer to use the plants while they are still fresh. However, this is often not practical, and good dyes can be made from plants which have been properly stored. Hang the bunches upside down in a dry shady area, (even a cool closet indoors will do) to await the proper time. Sumac, especially, dyes best when dried out weeks or months before use.

Another method is to store the refrigerated or frozen juices of the plant. First chop the fresh plant into two- or three- inch sections, just as you would do if you were preparing to dye right away. See details on page 28. Then boil the pieces in an enamel pot which is three-quarters full of plant material, with enough water to cover. Simmer or gently boil this mixture for one to two hours. It is not necessary to strain the juice. I invariably dye my wool in the pot with plant and all, as is done by the dyers in Scotland. This ensures a deeper color, and most plant materials can be removed from the dyed fleece or skeins easily enough. Besides, finding a tiny pokeberry seed or goldenrod bloom in one's knitting yarn can be enchanting!

Gallon milk cartons make ideal containers for dye juices. Quart or pint cartons or other vessels can be used if gallon-size is not available. Most frozen juices are as good as fresh when used many months later. I usually do not refrigerate juices longer than three months. If mold forms in the carton, this sometimes affects the dye color. Berries, too, can be stored in containers and frozen, although pokeberries store best dried.

The Mordant-Dye Combination

If you have gathered a specific plant, you may already know what mordant you will use on your wool. However, wool can be mordanted well in advance of dyeing. Mordant a small amount of wool beforehand in each of the common mordants. Then, when your dyebath is ready, you can obtain different colors in a relatively short time, by using each kind of mordanted wool in the same dye. It is the plant-mordant combination that determines the final color.

Sorting and preparing plants for dyeing. Long-stalked plants are hung up in bunches, until they can be chopped into shorter segments and boiled in a dyebath.

From the very beginning of your mordanting-dyeing procedure, keep a label on each batch of yarn or sample. If you forget what mordant you used (the mordant will not change the color of the wool perceptibly) you might easily come up with a brilliant green just when you wanted pale yellow. The label follows each lot of wool or experimental sample through all the processes, saving on many unpleasant surprises. A swatch of dyed wool should be stored away with this label at the end of the procedures, giving you enough information to closely duplicate the color at another time.

You will probably not be able to duplicate the color exactly because so many factors affect it. A drier fleece, for instance, will give a deeper color than one with a high oil content. The label should contain 1) the mordant, 2) the plant used for dye, 3) the date and place the plant was picked, and 4) any special times for cooking in the mordant or dyebath (see below). The place the plant grows is important because the dye may change with the mineral content of the soil. Goldenrod picked along a beach is very apt to give a different shade of yellow than goldenrod picked in a mineral-rich soil.

All mordants are metal based, and whether they are common household substances or metallic salts with fancy names, they introduce a foreign compound to the wool or other fiber that damages it to a certain extent. Therefore, the minimum amount of mordanting, as given in the recipes that follow, should be done, and only when that proves unsatisfactory should more of the chemical be added. Mordants also vary in their effects on different plants, and you must know by reading and experimenting what to expect from each plant-mordant combination. In general, however, it is safe to assume that plants which give dyes will give stronger and more lasting dyes with the addition of the proper mordant. Alum, probably the most commonly used mordant, will generally give the same color the plant gives with no mordant, but in a deeper, more brilliant shade.

Fixatives like vinegar and salt help penetration and therefore brighten the color. Salt is a neutral catalyst which speeds the dyeing.

The instructions that follow are meant for wool, the fiber that usually gives the best results. In general, animal fibers take deeper colors than plant fibers from the same vegetable dyes. Mohair and angora, for example, color vividly with most of the wool dyes. Silk, however, has a dyeing lore all its own, giving brilliant colors with some plants and none at all with others. If you are interested in dyeing silk or plant fibers such as cotton, ramie, or linen, learn about their special plant-mordant combinations from the books in the Bibliography.

MORDANTS AND ADDITIVES

The dyer turned to Mother Nature once again to solve the problem of running or fading dyes. And, as always, she provided. From the earth came mordants in the form of alum and various metal compounds; from the sea, salt; from plants came natural tannic acid in bark, nuts, and roots, and vinegar from grapes. American Colonial women, as we have mentioned, found their iron mordant in rusty nails, and they also used homemade vinegar. Today, we can buy all the common mordants and fixatives in grocery stores, pharmacies, or chemical supply houses (see the Sources of Supply at the back of the book).

Two simple fixatives can be found right in the kitchen. They are *vinegar* and *salt*. Although they do not produce very fast dyes, they are perfectly safe to use, even with small children, and give a variety of colors with different

Even the deep color of pokeberries is brightened and made fast by salt, the most commonly available fixative. When squashing berries to release the juice, some people use a spoon and some prefer to use their hands.

plant materials. A pinch of salt is often added to a berry dyebath to brighten the color.

Alum and *cream of tartar* are also common chemicals that have various uses in the home. Alum (potassium aluminum sulfate) can be purchased at a chemical supply house, and five pounds is a good supply, for it is frequently used. The alum found on pharmacy shelves is usually ammonium aluminum sulfate, which can be used nicely as a mordant, but will not guarantee fastness as will the potassium salt. Alum is often combined with cream of tartar (tartaric acid) to produce more luster in the dyed wool. Cream of tartar can be bought in small amounts in any grocery, but the two and a half pounds you will probably want to start with should be purchased from a chemical supply house. Alum alone or alum/cream of tartar gives a deeper-hued, longer-lasting color than unmordanted wool with the same plant dye.

Two commonly used mordants are the salts of *copper* and *chrome.* Iron and tin are also widely used (see below). When working with any of these mordants, caution must be employed, especially around youngsters, as some of the chemicals are poisonous and irritating to the skin. Chrome is the most dangerous — the fumes are noxious and the substance is corrosive to the skin. Work in a well-ventilated room, especially when the mordant pot is on, and wear rubber gloves. Chrome, in the form of potassium dichromate or bichromate, and copper sulfate can be purchased from a chemical supply house. Only one pound of each metallic mordant is necessary as they are used sparingly. They are harsh, and could cause damage to the wool. Chrome will develop many naturally yellow or orange dyes into bright shades of gold, orange, and rust. Good dark blues, purples, and even black dyes can be developed from natural deep pinks and lavenders. Copper is not quite as harsh as chrome. It is good for developing greens and browns from natural greenish-yellows and light green-browns.

Tannic acid (tannin) is a natural iron mordant in tree bark, oak galls, nut hulls, and some roots. Although not mentioned specifically in this book, it is often used as a mordant for cotton in combination with alum and cream of tartar. As a dye, it produces tan or light brown shades in wool and other fibers.

The salts of *iron* and *tin*, in addition to being used as regular mordants, are used as additives in small amounts in the dyebath itself. One pound each of iron, in the form of ferrous sulfate, and tin, in the form of stannous chloride, should be enough for a long time. Additives are used with unmordanted or alum, tannic-acid, or copper-sulfate mordanted wool. Each plant-mordant-additive combination then produces its own shade. Iron mordant or additive darkens the dye color, frequently producing muted shades of brown, green, or dark blue-black. Tin has almost the opposite effect, lightening and brightening. Its most spectacular results are on oranges, reds, and purples. When used as an additive, the effect of just a small pinch of iron or tin is immediately visible, and if the color change is not strong enough, more can be added — but only up to a limit, since iron and tin are particularly harsh on the wool. Iron dries it out, and too much tin can make it into a clinging spaghetti-like mass.

PREPARING A MORDANT BATH

Materials:
    laundry tub, filled with rainwater (optional)
    1 lb. washed fleece
    4–quart enamel pot, or one big enough to hold 3 gal. water and 1 lb. wool
    stove or hotplate
    sink or washtub
    small "postage" scale
    measuring spoons
    glass or enamel cup for dissolving mordant
    glass rod or stick for stirring
    hooked rod for lifting fleece from bath (an old soup ladle with a hook at the end of the handle is ideal)
    rubber gloves
    foil tray or other transport for fleece
    newspaper or paper towels, for splatters
    any of the mordants (alum, cream of tartar, chrome, iron, copper, tin, table salt, vinegar)

The basic mordant recipe is one pound of wool to three gallons of water, plus a small amount of any of the mordants (see below). It is probably worth mentioning the obvious fact that different mordants are not combined, except in the case of alum/cream of tartar, or, when used as additives, iron and tin, which combine with chemicals in a previous mordant.

If smaller quantities are used, as may be necessary in a classroom where only hotplates are available, cut recipes accordingly. For example, if you have only a two-gallon pot, use one gallon of water, ⅓ pound of fleece, and ⅓ the normal amount of mordant. The rest of the instructions are the same for any quantities.

Fill the pot with water from the rainwater tub. Soft rainwater is used to avoid adding unnecessary chemicals to the wool, which would either change the color slightly or block the process. If rainwater is impractical to collect,

Mordanting set-up includes: hot plate, large pot with stick for stirrer, bags and jars of mordants. In front are shown a kitchen implement with hooked handle and measuring spoons.

experiment with your own quantities. Don't use more than one on the following list at a single time!

3 oz. alum combined with 1 oz. cream of tartar

1 tbs. chrome

3 oz. copper sulfate (copper), sometimes called cupric sulfate

3 oz. ferrous sulfate (iron)

2 oz. stannous chloride (tin)

1½ cups salt

6 cups vinegar

In a glass or enamel cup, dissolve the mordant in a little warm water (except for the vinegar, of course, which can be added directly) and add the solution to the mordant pot. Heat bath to lukewarm (a comfortable hand heat), and add the fleece to it. Remember that the fleece must be thoroughly wet before going into the bath, so that mordanting right after washing the fleece is a logical time saver.

After adding the fleece, bring the bath to a boil, and then quickly turn down to a simmer. If using chrome, keep a lid on the pot during the entire mordanting process, because the chemical is sensitive to light and its fumes are poisonous. Simmer the fleece for one hour. Allow the bath to cool a little, and then remove the fleece with a hooked rod into a rinse bath. The water in the rinse (either tap or fresh) must be hot because, just as in washing, the fleece can be matted by a sudden change of temperature.

tap water is fine. But if your water supply is hard, make sure to add a softener to the water.

Next, measure out the mordant you have chosen. For three gallons of water the following amount of any one mordant is appropriate, although later on you may want to

After dissolving the required mordant in warm water, add it to the pot, heat bath to lukewarm, and add thoroughly wet fleece.

Remove the fleece from the rinse with the hooked rod, squeeze the excess water out, and place on the sink drainboard or a tray. The wool is now ready for the dyepot. If time runs out, hang the fleece to dry overnight, but remember to wet it again before it goes into the dyepot. Chrome-mordanted fleece must be dyed right away; however, the other mordants give better results the longer the wool is stored before dyeing.

Nature Dyeing

Once the plant material has been picked, sorted, and chopped, it is ready to yield its dye. In most cases, the best result will be obtained with fresh plants, but dried and stored material can also be used (see page 24). If the cooked juices have been frozen, they can be thawed, heated, and used as the dyebath without further preparation.

It is useful to think of plant materials in three categories: tender, fibrous, or woody. Tender dye plants include delicate leaves and flower parts and very ripe berries, fibrous dye plants include tough leaves and stems, and woody dye plants include twigs, branches, and nut hulls. Roots should be treated as either fibrous or woody, depending on how tough they are.

Simmer wool for an hour in the mordant pot, and then rinse in hot water. As long as it has been washed, wool can be mordanted and dyed in fleece or skein. Skeins are shown drying in the background.

Ragweed is thought of as a "fibrous" plant for the purposes of classifying it for dyeing procedures.

Dyeing set-up includes most of same equipment as mordanting set-up: hot plate, large pot with stick for stirrer, measuring spoons, and hook. A tray of marigolds will be simmered in the dyebath, producing yellow, orange, or gold shades depending on the mordant previously used on the wool.

PREPARING A DYEBATH

Materials:
 laundry tub filled with rainwater (optional)
 4-quart enamel pot
 enough plant material to fill pot ¾ full
 a small handful of fleece, mordanted or unmordanted (for larger quantities, one pound of wet wool to 3 gallons of water is about right)
 stove or hotplate
 sink or tub for rinse
 glass rod or stick for stirring
 hooked rod for lifting fleece from bath
 foil tray or other transport for fleece
 newspapers and towels for cleaning up

The first step in preparing a dyebath is soaking the plants. Plants of any category should be soaked at least overnight. Use the water you plan to use in the dyebath and enough plant material to fill your dyepot ¾ full. If the plant is fibrous, soak at least three days for optimum results. You will get dye from the plant if the soaking time is shorter, but it will be weaker than it might be. If the plant is woody, soak for a week. Walnut hulls, a common source of light brown, should really be soaked from two weeks to a month, although good results will be obtained with less time.

After the soaking, the plant material and its water must be cooked from one to two hours. Here again, the time varies with the type of plant. Tender or fibrous plants can cook for an hour, woody plants and mashed berries for at least an hour and a half. Elderberries and pokeberries, by the way, like salt while cooking. I use a half a cup to a three-gallon pot of berries. Additional water should be added to the dyepot to replace what boils away.

At the end of the initial boiling time, the plant material can either be left in the pot or removed, and the fleece or yarn added. I prefer to leave the plants and the wool together, sometimes called simultaneous dyeing , a method which is traditional for many dyers. Some of the plant material can be removed if the pot is too full.

Dyeing can be done in the skein after the wool has been spun. However it is easy to see that the dye will penetrate more quickly and thoroughly when dyed in the fleece, or wool. Perhaps that is how "dyed in the wool" came to mean "thorough" or "uncompromising." In all cases, the fibers must be clean and wet upon entering the dyebath.

It is *wrong* to put a small amount of fleece into the dyebath and then add to it. It must all be put in at once, otherwise the bit you put in first will begin to soak up the

Checking the color of wool in the dyebath.

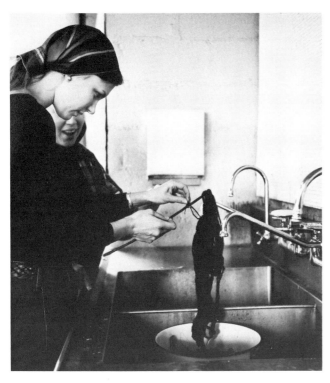

When the proper color has developed, rinse wool in hot water until rinse water runs clear.

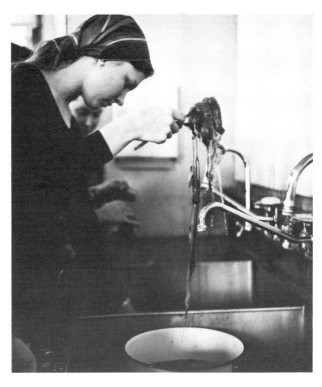

When rinsing is finished, the wool is ready for drying.

dye before the rest of it, and your fleece or yarn will not be evenly dyed, but come out various shades, the first-added wool being the darkest. All the wool goes in at once, is pushed under the dye juice, and gently stirred once or twice while dyeing to ensure even penetration of color. Do not put so much wool in the pot that it won't float, as wool in an overloaded pot will mat when it simmers. Room must remain in the pot for the wool to float a bit. One pound of wet wool to three gallons of water is the measure.

For the next hour, the ingredients must only *simmer*. Fibers, especially wool, can be ruined by overcooking. During this time, an additive of iron or tin can be included in the dyebath to darken or lighten the color that is emerging. Start with only one-quarter teaspoon and cook for five minutes before judging the result. If more is needed, add only a pinch at a time.

If the proper color is developed before the hour is up, stop dyeing and begin rinsing at that point. The dyebath can be used again for a second, or even a third, batch of wool, but the color will get lighter with each succeeding use of the same dyebath.

Once dyed, the finished product must be rinsed in hot water until the rinse water is clear, and then hung to dry. Naturally, the drying will take place fastest outdoors in full sun. However, some of the more delicate dyes will fade with such exposure. Pokeberry-dyed fibers, in particular, may fade immediately.

Some nature dyes will fade a little with exposure to sun. Why not let it happen while they are drying?

Goldenrod (at rear) will give a dye of yellow to greenish shades. Sumac (large leaves) gives shades of tan to brown. For more positive identification of these and other common dyeplants, see the field guide and its list on pages 16 -19 .

DYE PLANTS AND COLORS WITH DIFFERENT MORDANTS

Trees and Shrubs

Apple *(Malus)*: twigs; *no mordant:* yellow; *chrome:* orange; *alum/cream of tartar:* apricot.

Bayberry *(Myrica)*, also called Waxmyrtle; berries; *alum:* blue. North America.

Blackberry *(Rubus)*, also called Bramble; berries; *alum:* rose to pink.

Butternut *(Juglans cineria)*, also called White Walnut; hulls; *alum:* tan, brown. North America.

Cherry *(Prunus)*; twigs; *alum:* yellow to brown.

Elder *(Sambucus)*; berries; *alum* alone, or with *salt* or *vinegar:* violet, deep pink, green (with iron additive).

Grape *(Vitis)*; fruit; *alum:* lavender; *chrome:* red-purple.

Pear *(Pyrus)*; twigs; *no mordant:* yellow; *chrome:* orange, apricot.

Sumac *(Rhus typhina* or *R. glabra)*; berries — pick red berries only, the white-berried *R. vernix* gives a poison-ivy-like rash; *alum:* brown; *chrome:* tan. Dried leaves and stems; *alum:* tan, gray (with iron); *alum/cream of tartar:* soft brown.

Viburnum, Mapleleaf *(Viburnum acerifolium)*; berries; *alum/cream of tartar:* maroon; *chrome:* navy blue to black; *copper:* khaki.

Walnut *(Juglans nigra* or *J. regia)*; hulls; *no mordant:* tan, brown.

White Birch *(Betula papyrifera)*; inner bark — use only decaying bark from already-downed trees or branches; *no mordant:* tan.

Wild Plants and Weeds

Black-eyed Susan *(Rudbeckia)*, also called Coneflower; above-ground plant; *alum:* green, yellow; *chrome:* greenish gold.

Dandelion *(Taraxacum officinale)*; above-ground plant; *alum:* yellow to lime. If only the flowers are used, *alum:* yellow; *copper:* soft green.

Dock *(Rumex)*, also called Curly Dock; above-ground plant; *alum/cream of tartar:* soft gold, silver gray (with iron).

Evening Primrose *(Oenothera biennis)*, also called Common Evening Primrose; above-ground plant; *alum:* yellow; *chrome:* orange. Although common in the eastern United States, use moderation when picking in the western United States, leaving plenty of flowers to go to seed.

False Solomon's Seal *(Smilacina racemosa)*, also called False Spikenard; berries; *alum:* pink. Be very sparing in your use of this plant. Always leave enough berries so it can reseed itself. This is listed in America by the Wildflower Preservation Society as a wildflower that should not be picked or dug, at least near large towns and tourist points in the East. It is somewhat more common in the West.

An armful of goldenrod, sumac, and pokeberries, which yield reddish shades, and are not safe to eat.

Goldenrod *(Solidago)*; flowers; *alum:* yellow; *chrome:* deep orange; *iron:* yellow, green. If the entire above-ground plant is used, greener shades result with *alum* or *iron.*

Jewelweed *(Impatiens),* also called Touch-Me-Not or Snapweed; above-ground plant; *alum:* apricot; *chrome:* golden orange; *copper:* brown. North America.

Lamb's Quarters *(Chenopodium album)*; above-ground plant; *alum/cream of tartar:* soft green. North America.

Mullein *(Verbascum)*; above-ground plant; *alum:* gold.

Mustard *(Brassica),* also called Wild or Field Mustard; above-ground plant; *alum:* pale green; *chrome:* lime-gold.

Pokeweed *(Phytolacca americana)*; berries; *alum:* red, pink, gold (with copper), purple (with tin). North America.

Queen Anne's Lace *(Daucus carota),* also called Wild Carrot; above-ground plant; *alum:* yellow, gray (with iron); *chrome:* gold.

Ragweed *(Ambrosia)*; above-ground plant; *alum:* green. This is the plant that causes hayfever in those allergic to its pollen.

St.-John's-Wort *(Hypericum perforatum)*; above-ground plant; *alum:* yellow; *chrome:* deep yellow; *vinegar:* red.

Garden Flowers and Shrubs

Chrysanthemum; flowers; *alum:* yellow; *chrome:* gold, orange.

Coreopsis, also called Tickseed; flowers; *chrome:* burnt orange; *tin:* bright yellow.

Dahlia; flowers — red are the best; *alum:* yellow, gold; *chrome:* tan, orange-red.

Daylily; flowers; *alum;* yellow, apricot; *tin:* bright yellow; *chrome:* pale green.

Forsythia; stems, leaves, and *flowers; alum/cream of tartar;* butter yellow.

Iris; flower petals of purple iris; *alum:* light blue.

Marigold; flowers; *alum:* yellow; *chrome:* orange, gold.

Privet; leaves and stems; *alum:* light green; *copper or iron:* green.

Prepared Foods or Vegetables

Beets; juice; *no mordant* if juice is canned: pink; *alum* with fresh juice: *tan.*

Blueberries, also called Bilberries; frozen berries; *alum:* pale blue.

Carrots; tops; *alum:* lime green, yellow; *copper:* green. If carrot juice is used, *alum* yields apricot.

Onions; outer skins; *alum:* yellow; *chrome:* orange, golden-brown.

Spinach; leaves; *alum:* lime-yellow, green.

Continued on page 37

Natural wool colors. *Clockwise from left:* spotted sheep, brownish gray, dark gray, blended gray and white, Karakul, gray, white (grease), white.

Other natural fiber colors. *Clockwise from left:* yak and wool blend, unbleached linen, buff cashmere, opossum, zoo yarn (a blend of many animal fibers), Iran cashmere, cashmere blend, mohair, gray alpaca, angora, Karakul and mohair, tussah silk, Yorkshire terrier. See Chapter 5 for more information about these and other fibers.

Nature-dyed skeins of wool. *Clockwise from left:* ragweed green (alum mordant) with white blended in; walnut; indigo (alum); logwood; indigo and goldenrod (alum); goldenrod orange (chrome); onion skins (alum); goldenrod yellow (alum); cochineal red (alum); pokeberry pink, lamb's quarters (copper sulfate). See Chapter 2 for information about mordanting and dyeing.

Two purebred sheep, both white although the true color can be seen only on the shorn one.

After being sheared, fleece is sorted, teased, washed, and then hung to dry out of doors on a convenient tree.

A simmering pot of pokeberry-dyed fleece, alum mordanted. After berries are soaked overnight, they are cooked. A tablespoon or so of salt was added to the dyepot to brighten the color.

Spinning line flax with a right-side-up spindle, one that has the whorl at the top.

Combinations of colors can be made on the same skein or by top-dyeing. This skein is logwood dyed (without a mordant) on the bottom, while the top is prepared for tie-dyeing.

Commercial Dyestuffs

Indigo; water-soluble extract (it's blue) from the indigo plant dyes wool, cotton, silk shades of blue with *no mordant*. In the past, other preparations of indigo have been used, some of which are caustic, and vat-dyeing should only be used with more instruction on dyeing methods.

Cochineal; powder extract derived from an insect dyes wool and silk shades of red to purple. *Alum:* red; *chrome:* pink to purple; *tin:* scarlet; *iron:* maroon.

Madder; powder extract or dried root of the plant gives shades of orange and red to wool and silk. *Alum* or *chrome:* reddish orange; *tin:* orange.

Logwood *(Haematoxylon);* chips, crystallized extract, or hunks of the tree bark dyes wool and silk in shade of purple. *No mordant:* rose; *alum:* purple; *tin:* brilliant purple; *chrome:* navy blue.

3 When a Spinster Puts Her Cards on the Table

Cards

Roll log

Before you spin the fleece you have to card it, or soften it, like taking out the dirt that is in it. After you have carded the fleece it becomes into a roll log. Then it is ready to be spun.

When a spinster puts her cards on the table, this is not an invitation to bridge. Rather, she is preparing to brush her fleece into workable order for spinning, with two hand-held wire brushes called cards.

After the fleece has been sorted, picked, teased, washed, mordanted, dyed, and dried, the individual fibers are in a disorganized condition. They must be lined up roughly in the same direction, so that spinning, essentially a process of twisting arranged fibers together, can be done.

Depending on the quality of the fibers — long, short, rough, delicate, matted — various kinds of arranging are necessary. Basically, there are two ways to sort out fibers, one by carding and one by combing. Carding is a rough process, which pulls fibers in opposite directions in order to line them up. You can card by hand or on a machine, in which each of the cards is a revolving drum. Carding on the drum is even rougher than hand carding, and therefore is not used when preparing delicate wool such as Merino. On the other hand, very matted or coarse fleece is often carded first on the drum and then on the hand cards, or run through the drum twice.

Combing is what it sounds like — you draw a wire comb through the fibers, just as you would run a comb through your hair to smooth out the snarls. Combing further refines the arrangement of the fibers after carding, so that they are all nearly parallel. This is an advantage where the fibers themselves are long enough to be parallel for a significant amount of length, and where combing can remove any remaining short fibers. Only worsted-quality fleece is combed, after carding. If you buy combed wool for spinning, it will probably be called "top". This means that you have long fibers to start with (long "staple"), and that they are all arranged in a parallel order for spinning.

Flax is combed, never carded, because the fibers are so long. The flax you buy for spinning may be called "sliver" or "line flax". It is essentially the same as top, but comes in a thin strand. You can also buy flax "tow," which is composed of the shorter flax fibers that have been separated out from the line flax in the final combing.

With only a minimum of carding, and no combing, you can spin excellent yarn from the short fibers of a variety of animals and plants, as illustrated in the rest of the book. Carding does not finally leave the fibers parallel, as combing does. Instead, each fiber is bent or rolled, and it is the bent ends that are twisted together during spinning. This arrangement of unspun yarn is called "roving" when you buy it. I use the traditional term "rolag," which means roving but is a more picturesque word, for rolags look (and sound) like little rolled logs!

Hand Carding and Machine Carding

Early European cards were made from a plant, the fuller's teasel *(Dipsacus fulloneum),* whose dried round flower heads are covered with stiff, hooked spines like a pincushion. These spines could dig in and hold on to the tangled fleece. The term "teasing" wool, as in picking, comes

Carding fleece to prepare it for spinning.

39

from the name of the plant. Even the term "carding" is derived, in a round-about way, from the plant. The Latin *carduus* means thistle, and the teasel, looking a great deal like a thistle, was called *la cardère* by the French. Carding has been done, even by non-Europeans, in much the same way for centuries. Traditionally Navajo Indians used burrs attached to a board for carding, and primitive man may have carded with animal teeth attached to a hand-shaped backing. The American Colonists used six teasels, three on top and three on the bottom to card their wool.

Today we use cards of fine wire set at an angle in a leather or rubberized cloth, and mounted on a rectangular wooden board with a handle. Spinsters usually have two pair of cards, one for grease fleece and one for washed and dyed fleece.

It is best to be seated while carding. Mark one card with an L for lap, because it will rest in your lap with the wires pointing up. Hold the other card, called the free card, in your "best" hand, with the wires pointing down. If you are right-handed, hold the free card in your right hand, because this card does most of the work, and if you are left-handed, hold it in your left hand.

Place the fleece on the lap card, hooking it onto the bent wires in the middle of the card in only small amounts at one time. Now brush the free card, always in the same direction, from the top to the handle side of the lap card. It is an easier motion than you might think because the cards are always held far enough apart so that the wires do *not* mesh. You are carding the fleece atop the wires of the lap card, not the wires themselves. Experience will tell you when you have the right amount of fleece on the card (it's better to have too little than too much) and how far apart to hold the cards.

Placing fleece on the lap card, by hooking in small amounts at a time.

The free card does most of the work, never meshing with the wires of the lap card yet brushing the fleece on top of the lap card.

Note the bent wires on the cards, which help to hold and straighten the fibers.

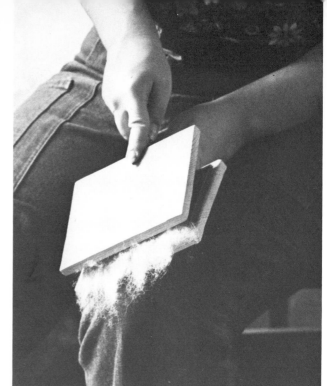

Card until the fibers lie straight and are no longer on the surface of the cards.

To transfer fleece from one card to the other, lift the fleece off one card with the wires of the other, in an almost scraping motion.

Rolling the fleece off the lap card to make a rolag for spinning.

Ready for spinning. The cards can be picked clean with a crochet hook before the next time they are used. Keep a set of cards for use only with grease fleece.

It's best to accumulate six or seven rolags before starting to spin.

Card until the fibers are lying straight and are below the surface of the wires. Then *transfer* the fleece to the free card by brushing deeply so that the wires mesh. In carding, the lap card is always the lap card, and the free card, which does the stroking, is always the free card; they are never reversed. After transferring the fiber from the lap card to the free card, transfer it back to the lap card again. You can now resume the stroking motion. Finally, to get all the brushed fleece, which is by now embedded in the wires, onto the surface to be rolled into a rolag, again transfer it from the lap card to the free card, and then back to the lap card.

Now you are ready to make a rolag. This is where the fibers assume their bent arrangement, by being rolled off the lap card in one piece. To roll the fleece, hold it down on the lap card with one hand, turn your free card wires *down*, and with the free card's wooden edge, tuck up the loose ends of the fleece under the thumb that is pressed against the wires of the lap card. Now place the free card wires on top of the fleece fold you have just made, press down and forward, rolling the fleece off the lap card.

Carefully picked fleece can be carded by machine, and yields larger rolags.

After the fleece is fed into the machine, it is automatically transferred from the small to the large drum.

Where large amounts of fleece require carding in a short time, a carding machine is nice to have around. Its two cylinders, covered with wire carding cloth, serve the same function as hand cards, but are mounted in such a way as to revolve by the use of a hand crank. The large drum is sometimes called the main cylinder or swift; the small one is sometimes called the feed roll or licker-in.

Never card grease fleece on a drum. It is harder on the wires, which are more costly to replace than those on hand cards and, once grease fleece gets the drums dirty, the carding machine cannot ever again be used for washed fleece. You can clean the remaining strands of fiber from either carding machine or hand cards by picking them off with a crochet hook. However, the grease from the grease fleece is impossible to remove.

To operate the carding machine, feed washed and well-picked fleece onto the small cylinder by way of the metal tray, or feed pan. Take care not to jam the drums by feeding in too much fleece at one time. As the drums revolve, the fleece is transferred to the larger drum by the pulling action of the wire cloth, which also untangles the fibers and removes foreign matter. When all the fleece is transferred, the carding is finished. In this manner, as much as three pounds of fleece can be carded in one hour.

If you are going to continue carding the fleece on hand cards, remove the fleece in one long strip from the drum, and make sure to hook it on the hand cards so you will continue to card in the same direction. You will have to lift up a part of the fleece on the drum to obtain a free end, and work it off from there. If you are making a rolag, start rolling from this free end, which can be picked up with a knitting needle, in the same way as on the hand cards.

Carding can serve two purposes at one time because it is also a way to blend fibers or colors together before spinning. Try carding unusual materials together to blend them — even small feathers and wool, if you are feeling adventurous! Blending should be distinguished from plying (see page 61) in which separate strands of yarn are spun together, and from weaving together different fibers, as in linsey-woolsey, where the warp is linen and the filling is wool.

When all the fleece is transferred, carding is finished. Fleece can be removed with the aid of a knitting needle.

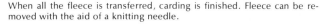

Rolags are made by hand. The drum can be cleaned with a crochet hook. Carding machines should never be used for grease fleece.

4 Spindle Whorls & Spinning Wheels

Spindal

Spinning wheel

After you have made the fleece into roll logs you spin it with a spindal or a spinning wheel
when you start spinning with a spindal so you don't forget your steps if you whant you could say this Pinch Pull Slide.
After you have spun, you are ready to weave.

High in the mountain villages of Greece, along the cloud-touched slopes of the South American Andes, on the dry plains of the Sudan, in the deserts of Arabia, and amidst the flame-colored rocks of the American Southwest, the primitive hand spindle is still used to make yarn.

Although for thousands of years man has begun his cloth-making process with this small tool, which serves as a weight and a holder for the raw fibers that have been transferred into one continuous strand, there came a time when the increased demand for cloth turned inventive minds to seeking faster methods of production.

It was in India, centuries ago, that the hand spindle assumed a horizontal rather than vertical position, and was made to turn not by a simple twirl of man's hand but by the turn of a larger wheel, which added greater efficiency to the spinning system and great speed to the now horizontal spindle.

I have never met a man, woman, or child, who, once exposed to handspinning, has not found it to be intriguing. The turning of whorl or wheel casts a soothing spell upon the beholder. Youngsters especially enjoy the aspect of creating something usable from the rawest materials, and anyone can find a personal link to history in spinning. The hand spindle, in much the same form as we use it today, goes back to the Stone Age! As far back as the days of the Egyptian dynasties, the familiar spindle with the whorl at the top instead of the bottom was already being used. The Greeks, too, accounted spinning very highly, as in the myth of the three Fates, who spun the thread of life itself, and the story of the unfortunate Arachne, whose spinning and weaving rivalled that of the goddess Athena. For her pride, Arachne was turned into a spider — the spinner who still outdoes us all.

Ready to Spin

As Stone Age man took readily available materials to fashion his first spindle, any student of spinning should learn to use what is at his fingertips: some clay and a pencil. Into a golf-ball sized lump of clay, insert a pencil so that the point end protrudes one inch from the other side. Tie on a piece of yarn, 18 to 24 inches long, just above the clay ball (on the side toward the shaft) with a tight double knot. Now loop a piece of yarn over the pencil point, bring it around the clay weight, up to the eraser, and loop it again.

A homemade "Stone-Age" type of spindle consists of a pencil and lump of clay. Some yarn is tied above the ball, looped around the pencil point, and then looped at top of pencil.

Spindles are used in many parts of the world, and are easy to make. *From left to right:* handcrafted "cookie" spindle, handcrafted small drawer-knob spindle, handcrafted medium drawer-knob spindle, handcrafted "Spinster" spindle (designed by author), Navajo Indian spindle, Sudanese spindle, traditional spindle. These last three, courtesy, of Clemes and Clemes, are used with whorl down; the others are used as pictured, with whorl up. The first two spindles at left, being relatively small, are good for thin yarns. "Spinster" spindle is especially good for thick yarns.

This serves as a leader for the unspun fibers (see below). The rolag is opened up at one end by pulling out a wide strand of fibers, and the other end is placed over the shoulder, arm, or wrist, to keep it out of the way of the spindle. Two hands are necessary for spinning, one to twist the spindle, and one to hold the unspun fibers. You will probably want to use your strongest hand for the twisting.

Now that you are in position to spin, you must learn to "fan" the fleece from the rolag. The fan is the opening up of the rolag between the fingers holding the unspun fibers and the beginning of the twisted yarn. This fan-shaped area is most important in controlling the amount of fibers drawn into the twist. Ideally, the amount should remain the same in order to produce even yarn. An experienced spinster controls her "draws" from the fan skillfully enough to produce thick-spun or thin-spun yarn at will. A heavier spindle is preferable for the spinning of thick yarn.

Both on hand spindles and wheels, a bit of already spun fiber is needed to get the spinning started, and it takes practice to make a smooth transition from this leader. Take the end of the yarn you looped around the spindle, and overlap it an inch or two on the fan. With both sections held firmly, give the pencil a twirl or two until the fleece can be felt twisting between your fingers. Yarn and rolag are now one. Instead of overlapping yarn and rolag, some people unravel the end of the yarn and mix the unspun fibers with it to produce a more even splice.

To continue spinning, twirl the pencil again, always in the same direction. Most people will be twirling with their right hands, so that the spindle and yarn twist in a clockwise direction. Technically this is called Z twist, because the fiber is twisted from left to right, as one would write a Z. If you are twirling with the left hand, you will be producing a twist in the opposite direction, called an S twist because the fiber is twisting from right to left, as one would write an S (counterclockwise). For all purposes, these twists are equivalent, but you should know the names for further reading.

After twirling the pencil, use the same hand to pinch and pull down the yarn just below the fan. This will pull more fibers into the twist ("drafting"). Let the yarn go, and twirl the pencil again. With practice you will be able to keep the pencil twirling smoothly and steadily, and not so hard that it flies up or to the side.

I mastered the hand spindle by repeating aloud, "Twirl, Pinch, Pull, Let Go!"

Once a floor-length strand of yarn has been spun, unloop it from the top of the pencil, and wind it in just above the clay ball. Now loop the yarn over the top of the pencil

Proper position for fanning the fleece. The lower hand pulls the fibers, in "draws," into the twist.

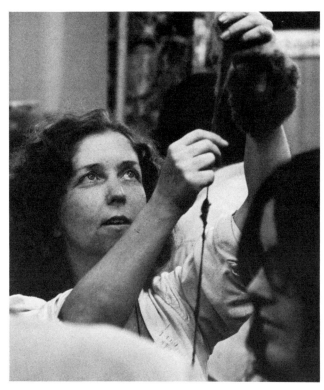

Spinning in progress. Note how the rolog is kept out of the way around the wrist or arm.

To continue spinning, twirl the pencil again.

Twirl, pinch, and pull for a good yarn.

again, and repeat the spinning procedure. As you spin, you will accumulate enough yarn to reach the upper perimeter of the clay ball and go up the shaft of the pencil-spindle until it is just under the eraser. The yarn roll should be thickest just above the clay ball and taper to a point under the eraser for the best balance. When this point has been reached, roll the yarn off the spindle into a ball, leaving enough on the pencil to form a new leader.

The spindle you have made with the pencil and clay ball is a free or drop spindle; the twisted fibers are kept at tension by the force of gravity. Some peoples, including the Greeks and the Navajo, traditionally used a spindle that rested on the ground over the thigh. The Navajo spindle consisted of a wooden shaft with a wooden disk slipped over it and attached one quarter of the distance from the bottom. Delicate fibers that won't support the weight of a whorl are spun traditionally with a supported spindle.

A workshop project in school or at home might be to make a "right-side-up" drop spindle, one where the whorl is at the top. The method of spinning is the same as already described, but the yarn has to be attached only at the top of the spindle, leaving the whole shaft for winding up the newly spun yarn. Try making one from a wooden dowel, a wooden knob such as those used on drawers for pulls, and a small metal hook with a screw attachment, like a cup hook. The dowel should be about 12 to 14 inches long for a medium-sized knob, and longer the larger the knob is. Make sure the width of the dowel is appropriate for the size of the hole in the knob. Any sort of knob will do as long as it is of wood, and has some depth to it for weight.

Apply a little Elmer's glue or similar white glue to the hole and dowel. Insert the dowel into the already centered hole of the knob, let dry, then screw the hook into the exact center of the knob top. When your spindle is assembled, tie and loop a yarn leader around the dowel right under the drawer knob, and pass the end of the yarn through the hook. You are ready to spin.

Spinning Wheels and How to Use Them

The spinning wheel, for all its complex wheels, shafts, flyers, pulley belts, and treadles, is not so very different from the hand spindle, which performs two basic operations: it allows the fiber to be twisted (spinning) and allows the spun yarn to be wound up (spooling). In its early forms the spinning wheel merely made these separate functions more efficient. Then, after centuries of development, a wheel was invented that made spinning and spooling simultaneous.

Make this spindle yourself. All you need is a drawer knob, some white glue or cement, a hook, and a dowel.

The spinning wheel does what the hand spindle does, but more efficiently. It twists fibers and provides a place for spun yarn to be wound up.

Spinning with a "right-side-up" spindle, similar to the kind that was used in ancient Egypt. Yarn is attached under whorl, and passed through hook.

The spinning wheel literally started from the ground up. It was a low wheel, at which the spinner knelt or sat on the ground, and was first devised in India during the early Christian Era, for spinning cotton and other plant fibers. In this wheel, called a Charkha, the spindle was mounted horizontally, and attached to a big wheel by a looped cord fitting into the groove on the spindle whorl and then into the rim of the wheel. By turning the wheel just a little, either by hand or by a hand crank, the spindle could be made to turn a great deal — the same principle as a gear system. Fiber to be spun was first attached to a piece of yarn already on the spindle-shaft tip, and then was fed from the fan into the twist, as on the hand spindle. When an arm's length of yarn was spun, the large wheel was reversed, in order to spool the yarn onto the spindle shaft. Then spinning was resumed.

The Indian wheel, which can still be found in use, gradually diffused to Europe from Asia, around 1300. The Europeans adapted it to a sturdier construction for spinning wool and flax, rather than the more delicate cotton, silk, and hemp fibers, and raised it from the ground to a bench. Where this type of wheel is still used it is called the wool wheel or the great wheel.

It took the inventive genius of Leonardo da Vinci to draw up plans for a wheel that both twisted the fibers and wound the finished yarn onto a spool, or bobbin, in one process. But it was not until 1530 that such a wheel was actually produced and put to use by a German woodworker, Johann Jürgen. The new improvement was the flyer, a wishbone-shaped arc of wood mounted on the spindle shaft. The flyer revolves on one pulley, the bobbin, within its arms on another pulley. The yarn is threaded from the bobbin, over a hook or slit in the flyer arm, through a hole on the side of the spindle shaft, and then through the tip of the front end of the spindle shaft. The whirling flyer spins the yarn, while the bobbin, moving independently, winds it up.

Leonardo da Vinci helped invent the flyer on the spinning wheel — the arc-shaped wood or metal piece with holes, which is what makes spinning and spooling simultaneous.

A weedbag with swamp grass in it. The fringe and light stripes are dyed with madder, the dark center stripes are pokeberry (mordanted with alum), and the rest is undyed or dyed with walnut hulls. There are two thin stripes of goldenrod green near the base.

A doily, handspun, dyed, and crocheted by students. The center area is undyed grease yarn, the middle ring is undyed washed yarn, the outer rim is goldenrod yellow.

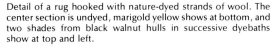

Detail of a rug hooked with nature-dyed strands of wool. The center section is undyed, marigold yellow shows at bottom, and two shades from black walnut hulls in successive dyebaths show at top and left.

Detail of crocheted afghan showing deep pink from pokeberries (alum), shades of blue and gray from indigo, gold from mullein (alum), tan from the inner bark of the white birch, walnut brown, and purple from logwood bark (alum). The white is undyed yarn.

A branch weaving by students, warped on a dowel and maple branch and suspended in a bent wild-grape-vine loom, which also serves as a hanger. The orange (onion skin with alum) and dark blue (indigo) are from handspun, nature-dyed yarns; the light blue is commercial angora.

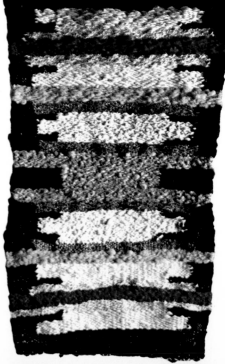

Another branch weaving by a student, with commercial and homespun yarns. See Chapter 6 for an introduction to weaving techniques.

Navajo-loom weaving by students. The yarns are handspun Greek mountain sheep and Haitian cotton, in nature-dyed and natural shades. Black, a sometimes difficult color to achieve, was obtained from chrome-mordanted, logwood-bark dyed yarn.

The last improvement before mechanized spinning was a treadle drive for the flyer wheel, invented around 1500 in Europe and around 1640 in China. The familiar traditional spinning wheel is this sort; it also has a distaff, which is a vertical post for holding flax fiber, mounted on the bench. The directions that follow are for the treadled flyer wheel, which, in addition to being a fast and efficient way to spin, allows you to ply yarn easily by reversing the wheel's rotation.

LEARNING TO TREADLE

Handling a spinning wheel has been compared by some of my students to "rubbing one's tummy while patting one's head." That is to say, coordination between hand and foot movements is necessary to successful operation of the wheel. So the first thing you must learn to do is *treadle*. This comes easier to some than to others. Young-

Spinning wheels, from left to right: broke-type tension, single-band wheel, made in New Zealand; Saxony-type replica, made in Germany; "gossip" wheel, made in Poland; antique Quebec wheel; Scotch-type wheel, made in Scotland.

sters, used to daily bike peddling, seem to take right to it. A certain rhythm must be established, and to achieve this, one of my lady students had to sing aloud, "Mary had a little lamb, little lamb, little lamb."

The dedicated spinster, or spinner, always removes one shoe before treadling. This makes for a better feel of the treadle, and also preserves the wood. Some old wheels have grooves worn into the wooden foot treadle, caused by years of "shoe treadling." Once the shoe is off, you should practice treadling with no yarn on the bobbin. When a rhythm is achieved with the treadling, and the wheel no longer goes into reverse, it is time to "thread up." The wheel always goes in the direction you push it to begin with — this should be away from the spindle and flyer for spinning, and in the other direction for plying. The treadling motion remains the same for both directions.

Learning to treadle and feed fiber into the twist requires much coordination. Each student first handles a single operation. Note that the treadler has removed his shoe, for a better "feel."

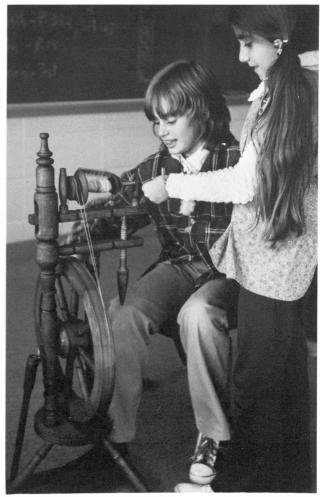

The treadler starts the wheel by turning one of the spokes clockwise. The motion of the flyer and bobbin can be seen clearly.

Threading the spinning wheel. Already spun yarn from the bobbin is pulled through a slit in the flyer, with the aid of a crochet hook.

SOLOING ON THE FLYER WHEEL

The leader yarn of about 14 to 18 inches long is tied onto the bobbin, then over a hook or slit in the flyer arm, then into an orifice on the top of the metal spindle shaft, and out through the orifice at the front end of the spindle shaft. This threading is easily done with the aid of a crochet hook. As spinning proceeds, you will learn to keep yarn take-up even by changing the hook or slit on the flyer that the yarn first goes through. And after spinning, you can manage to leave the same piece of yarn attached to the spindle for use when you next begin to spin. Now the rolag, prepared as in hand-spindle spinning, is joined to the leader. Lay the yarn atop one end of the rolag, and allow the unspun fibers to be drawn slowly into the twist as you treadle.

After that, it is threaded through two holes, called orifices, in the spindle shaft.

There is a different feel to the wheel when the bobbin is empty, as in your practice treadling, and when the yarn is twisting and being drawn in. And so it is advisable for the student spinner to treadle a bit while a more experienced partner handles the rolag. Once the treadler has the rhythm, he changes places with the feeder until each can handle both jobs. It is then time for one partner to coordinate foot and hands, and spin solo.

When you spun on the hand spindle, your hands stayed approximately in the same place while the fiber from the draft slipped between them — the weight of the whorl plus the pull from your free hand pulled the fibers into the twist. In the flyer wheel, the take-up motion of the spooling draws in the fibers similarly, so that your hands can also rest in about the same place throughout spinning. However, on a high wheel, they move back with the

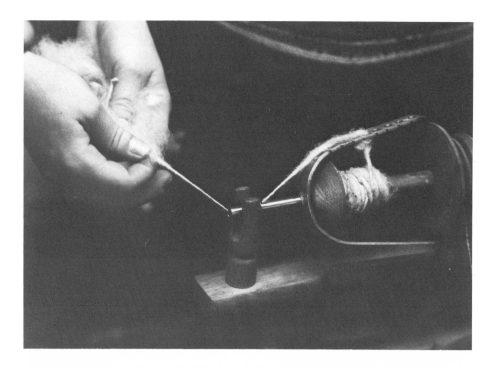

Ready to spin. This shows correct position of hands, making the fan, while spinning wheel is stationary.

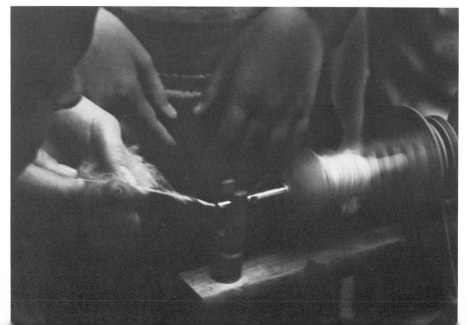

Correct position of hands, taking draws of yarn, while wheel is in motion.

Spinning solo after coordination of hand and foot movements has been mastered.

twisted fibers, until a sufficient length of yarn has been spun to be wound up in a separate operation.

On the flyer wheel, it is easy to ply two strands of yarn together. If the single strands of yarn have an S twist, the plying is in the Z-twist direction, which avoids overtwisting the yarns. Plying actually untwists the single strands a little, and can be used to correct slightly overtwisted yarn. As plying increases yarn strength, it is a good technique for some of the unusual fibers we will discuss in the next chapter. The techniques for plying are the same as for spinning a single strand, except that the motion of the wheel is reversed. Instead of a rolag to feed fibers into the twist, two strands of yarn from skeins or balls are fed through your fingers, with even tension on each strand, after attachment to the leader on the bobbin.

5 Natural Fibers from Plants & Animals

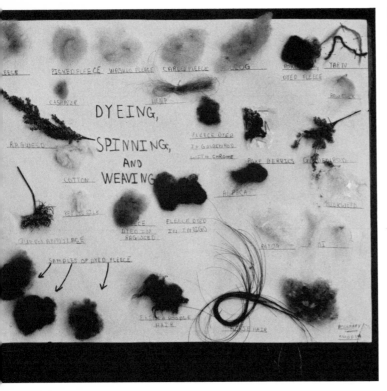

Rarely do we give thought to the plants and animals which provide the fibers in the clothes we wear. Cotton and wool are so common, and have been used throughout the world for so long, that we often forget fibers that have been the mainstays of the wardrobe and domestic textiles in other places and other times. Flax, of course, is still used, to make linen, and camel's-hair coats and mohair scarves from goat's hair are common items of apparel. But how about a scarf finer than mohair, made by the Eskimos from musk-ox hair, called *quiviut*? Or delicate and supple cloth from pineapple leaves? And closer to home, the shed hair of your favorite pet can be carded with wool to make very satisfactory yarn with a unique quality.

Today, due to scientific and technological advances, man is also able to create fibers synthetically. Yet with all their advantages, these new fibers cannot entirely replace the natural ones. Animal fibers of all sorts, including silk, take natural dyes with a brightness and luster that are often impossible to achieve with synthetics. Plant fibers, although they sometimes dye more palely, have subtle and varied textures that synthetics can never quite match, and are economically very important in nonindustrial countries for the manufacture of ropes, twines, sacking, and matting.

Fiber plants are either bast or nonbast. Bast is the long fibrous inner part of the stem of flax, ramie, jute(bark has bast), hemp, and other plants. Ramie is of a softer texture and shorter staple than the other bast fibers, and is fun to spin, especially for beginners.

Cotton and kapok come from hairy parts attached to seeds, and therefore are nonbast fibers. Cattail fluff and milkweed silk (North America), which are also parts of seeds, can be carded into other fibers and spun that way. Leaves yield fibers, too, including sisal from the agave, abacá from the banana, and coir from the outer husks of coconuts. Ramie, hemp, jute, and sisal are used primarily for industrial purposes. Sisal, which is difficult but possible to spin on a spindle or wheel, is still used in Latin America for heavy cloth as well as ropes or twines.

Animal sources range far and wide, from beasts of burden domesticated at the dawn of history to creatures of the wild. The ever-wandering sheep, the unassuming goat, the haughty camel and his cousins the llama, alpaca, and vicuña, and that Easter pet, the rabbit, all provide us with luxurious garments. These fibers are often carded together to produce interesting *undyed* colors and varied textures. Horsehair, buffalo hair, dog hair, even fur from the opossum, raccoon, and mink are most frequently used in combination with wool, but can be spun alone.

Silk comes from an animal source, the cocoons of the silkworm moth. The insect has been domesticated for centuries — just like sheep or goats! Since each cocoon unreels into a single long filament, fiber from this source is twisted, or "thrown," rather than being spun. However, the handspinner can obtain waste silk from the reeling process, or broken cocoons, and each of these have shorter fibers that can be spun very enjoyably.

Cotton

Have you ever wondered what fabric was used to wrap the Egyptian mummies? Chances are that the one you saw was wrapped in handspun *cotton*. For of all the plant fibers spun by man, cotton is one of the very oldest. Cotton remnants dating back seven thousand years have yielded their secrets to scientists who found them in caves: cotton was cultivated long ago in India, Mexico, Africa (including Egypt), and the Eastern countries. When Columbus discovered the new world, he found cotton already growing in the Bahamas. Since the time when Americans first cultivated cotton in Virginia, it has become a leading crop in the United States. Russia, China, and India are also large cotton producers.

Driving through or flying over America's "cotton belt" in summer, one can see miles and miles of white fields. The warmth of the sun pops open the brownish cotton bolls, really seed heads, to reveal a mass of white fibers ready for picking. Although once a hand industry on the plantations in the South, now machines take over when nature's job is done, picking, sorting out the numerous seeds, carding, spinning, weaving, and dyeing the finished cotton cloth.

The bulk of the world's cotton has fibers about one-half to three-quarters of an inch long. Extremely long staples are sometimes about one and a half inches long, such as those of pima or Egyptian cotton, both of which are natu-

An assortment of handspun fibers from animals and plants. The bumps are called slubs, and can be produced or not as the spinner chooses. *From top:* wool, bulky spun; grease wool, thin spun; alpaca; cashmere; gray angora; camel's hair; mohair; Yorkshire terrier; yak hair and wool, two-ply; silk; cotton, thin-spun; cotton, bulky-spun; linen; cot-lin, a blend of cotton and linen.

rally brownish in color. Absorbent cotton (cotton wool) used around the home is made from chemically treated fibers too short for industrial spinning, but give it a try, if you want to practice.

Because cotton fibers are very short in staple compared with wool, which ranges up to 15 inches or more, they must be handled with delicacy by the handspinner. For very fine threads, it is best not to use a dropped spindle, as the weight cannot be supported by the thread. Instead, a lightweight spindle supported in a bowl is used. The handspinner can get cotton right from the gin, a machine which removes the seeds and other foreign matter.

Unprepared cotton must be scoured to remove the natural wax before any dye will take, and even then special mordants are required if the dye is not to be several shades paler than on animal fibers. Indigo, however, is the cotton dye *par excellence,* and has been used for ages in Africa, South America, and the Orient. It gives several shades of blue without a mordant.

Flax and Other Bast Plants

If the mummy you saw was not wrapped in cotton, it might have been wrapped in *linen.* When civilization began, linen was already a major textile in Egypt, just as wool was in Mesopotamia, cotton in India, and silk in China. Flax, the plant that gives us linen, has been cultivated since the Stone Age, both for its seeds, which can be used for food and linseed oil, and for the bast fibers in its stem, which are so long that exceptionally fine yet strong thread can be spun from them.

In American Colonial days, before sheep became plentiful, every farmer had a flax patch of some half an acre, and most of the family's clothing was of linen or linsey-woolsey. After the invention of the cotton gin in 1794, which increased cotton production enormously, linen became less popular. It could never be adapted to machine processing as easily as cotton was. Russia produces most of the world's flax fiber now, and the finest linens are spun in Ireland and Belgium. The linen produced in this country is used for twine, toweling, and netting such as needlepoint canvas.

Flax undergoes some difficult processing before it is ready to spin, and on farms in many lands, even in today's mechanized world, these procedures are still done by manual labor. First, because length of fiber is so important, the entire plant is pulled up by the roots when ready for use. The plants are then tied in bundles, cured, and threshed between two smooth rollers or "rippled" to remove the seeds. In rippling, the bundle of flax is drawn through a coarse comb. Next, the outer stem is rotted away by soaking in water for ten days or more. This "retting," as it is called, decomposes the outer part of the stem to expose the bast fibers. Afterwards the flax is washed and spread on the grass to dry and bleach in the sun. Because flax is not very absorbent, and thus cannot be dyed easily, it is often further bleached to white, from its natural brownish color, before being woven. Next the flax is "scutched," or beaten against a board to remove what remains of the outer stem. Finally, it is "hackled," or pulled through a metal comb to remove the shorter fibers, the tow, and prepare it for spinning.

Rippling, retting, scutching, and hackling are used on the other bast fibers, too. *Jute,* originally native to India, produces fiber strands six to ten feet long in this fashion, which go to make burlap and sacking. Although not very durable, they are quite easily dyed to the brilliant colors you see so often in commercial burlap products. *Ramie,* sometimes called China grass, or grass linen, is not so tough a bast plant, and therefore is not retted. Instead, it

Irish line flax. Length of staple and stiff but pliable quality of fiber are unmistakable.
Note how the fibers all run parallel, as a consequence of combing.

is crushed, scraped, and washed to free the fibers and degum them. The resulting strong, lustrous fiber sometimes reaches 20 inches, although it's generally about six inches, and is mostly used in Asia and the Philippines.

Flax for spinning can be obtained in long fibers called line flax, which are sometimes a yard long, although the average is about 12 inches, and in the shorter flax tow, which is combed out of the line flax during hackling. Line flax is customarily spun from a distaff, which can be hand held for spindle spinning, used free-standing, or attached to a wheel, as previously mentioned. In working with groups on the hand spindle, I simply divide the bundle of flax fibers into slivers, pull them out a bit lengthwise, and commence with the spinning, as with wool. One big difference in spinning flax is that the fingers you draw with must be kept moist. This aids in setting the twist and smoothing the yarn. This procedure may also be helpful in spinning jute.

Spinning flax slivers. The fingers you draw with must be kept moist.

Native American Plant Fibers

Two plant fibers not commonly spun, but interesting and rewarding to work with, are *milkweed silk* and *cattail fluff.* Long ago, the Indians of America combined these fibers with wool and goat hairs in their spinning. It is difficult on crisp autumn days not to be aware of the tall milkweed growing alongside the road. The tough pods have burst open and are about to release their treasure of silken-winged seeds. This is the time to pick the pods, remove the silk hairs, and card them together with wool fiber. The brown seeds attached to the hairs usually fall off themselves as you prepare the fiber for spinning. Such a combination of half wool, half seed hairs makes for a soft, lustrous yarn.

When the velvety heads of the stately cattail overripen and burst, the fine short fibers cling to the mother plant over an entire winter. The durability of these seed hairs, and their ability to shed water, can be seen in the spring when they are unharmed after so much exposure to the elements. I find and collect them in the spring, and create a soft tweedy yarn by combining them with wool fibers during the carding process. Milkweed seed hairs usually fly away on the wind, rather than clinging to the pod over the winter. But they are durable too, and I have successfully washed yarns containing them.

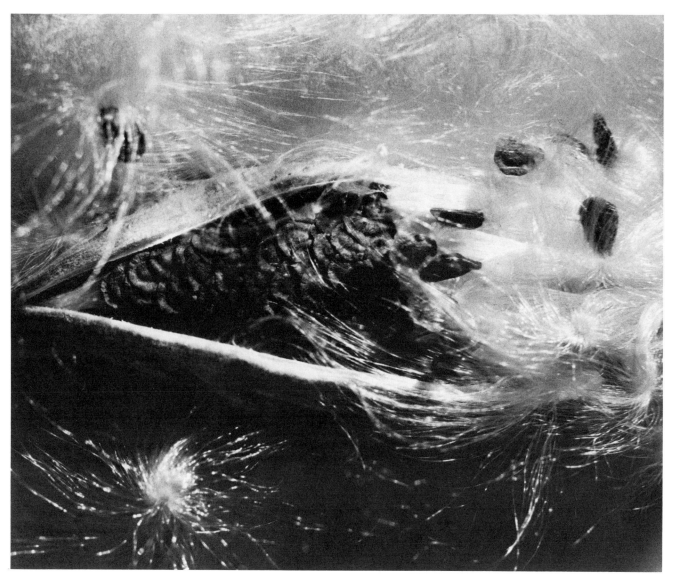

Milkweed silk, actually seed hairs from the ripe pod, can be spun up with wool for a silky, durable yarn.

A Spinster's Best Friend

Friendly, Angel, Poor Boy, Funnyface, Hansel, and Gretel comprise my *angora rabbit* family. They are purebred English and German angoras who provide me with pleasure, companionship, and fibers to spin. "Gathering" of angora wool, as it is called, varies from breeder to breeder. Some "pluck" their rabbits every three months, a process that doesn't hurt the animal at all. You just rapidly and gently tug on the coat, and the loose hairs come out in your fingers. Some of these silky fibers are five inches long. Others clip the hair with a scissors twice a year. I pluck my rabbits every two weeks, gathering at the most, one quarter of an ounce of wool from each rabbit. I save this until I have enough to spin up a skein — about three ounces, or a small bagful.

Angora rabbit fiber requires no carding. Merely fluff it up in your hand and start spinning (see picture on contents page). The finished yarn is remarkably strong, and is quite prized by needleworkers. A lovely combination can be made of angora and sheep's wool or alpaca while carding.

Gathering angora fiber does not disturb the animal in the slightest.

This gentle angora rabbit provides a very soft fiber that does not have to be carded before spinning. Actual spindle spinning of angora fiber is shown on the contents page.

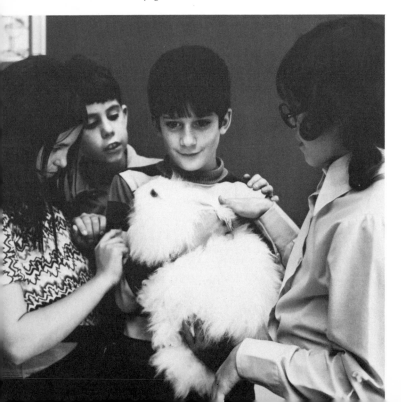

I herd my sheep with, and spin the hair of, my *Yorkshire terrier,* a delightful breed of dog which originated in Yorkshire, England. His hair is three to three-and a-half inches long, and I have carded and spun it alone, plying it to make a strong but rather coarse yarn. I also card it with wool for a soft, tweedy blend.

If you own a *Samoyed* dog, you can spin his hair alone, without the necessity of combining it with wool. Some durable and attractive fabrics have been woven of the white or cream color hair, which blends a soft, close undercoat with a straight, coarser overcoat.

Nearly everyone has a dog or cat in the house. Your pet would appreciate the extra grooming you give him, and you can use the hairs removed by the brush or comb for spinning. Especially in the spring, when animals shed their long winter coats, it is much nicer to spin the hairs than to have them all over the rug and upholstery. And wouldn't it be nice to wear a scarf or sweater of your favorite French poodle, cocker spaniel, or collie? Even Rex, the German shepherd, my four cats, and the bantam chickens here at home do not escape being "spun up" with the sheep's fleece. Everyone contributes to the fiber collection, and nothing is wasted.

In working with pet hair, the longer the fiber, the stronger and thinner the yarn can be spun. If the hair is very short, you will still be able to spin it alone after you are experienced, but it is not advisable to use this yarn for anything more than a decorative piece. Short hairs, however, can be combined with wool or other long fibers during carding to produce a yarn with the unique quality of your pet's hair, yet with strength enough for wearability.

A crocheted hat and scarf by the student, made primarily from yarn of French poodle hair blended during carding with wool. The hat also contains yarn dyed with logwood bark.

Camel's Hair

Hand gathering and sorting the soft inner hair from the coarse outer hair is also practiced on the two-humped camel (bactrian), whence comes the lovely tan *camel's hair* cloth. The Arabs also use the hair of the single-humped dromedary. The camel supplies them with clothes, blankets, and even tents. In spring, when the camel sheds, it looses its fur so fast and in such quantities that the coat hangs in ragged lumps. Yet the necessity of sorting out the scarce, fine undercoat of the bactrian make camel's hair a luxury.

The South American branch of the camel family includes the domesticated llama and alpaca, cousins to the camel, and fellow beasts of burden, and the more wild guanaco and vicuña. The fiber of the alpaca is the one most commonly used here, although the natives of the Andes also prize the shorter, coarser hair of the llama. Both these animals are naturally black, brown, buff, gray, or white, and gradation of subtle natural shades can be made by combining the colors while carding.

Goat's Hair

From the angora goat we get a ten-inch long, silky fiber which is spun into *mohair*. Its luster and strength are excellent, it takes dyes brilliantly, and is quite color fast. The white curly hairs are intermixed with much shorter fibers that don't dye at all. In the finer grades of mohair, these have been combed out, along with the shorter lengths of the other hairs.

While these goats originated in Turkey (angora and Ankara are really the same word), today Texas leads the world in mohair production. Turkey and South Africa are also homes for the goats.

From Kashmir, between India and Pakistan, originally came the long-haired goat that provides us with, of course, cashmere. The goat, which is white, tan, gray, or black, is raised in Tibet and India (some in Europe), where the women spend many days hand-sorting a sheared or combed fleece. They separate the coarse outer hairs from the soft fiber of the undercoat, which is only one to three-and-a-half inches long, but is exceptionally fine, although not very strong. An average goat only yields about three ounces of cashmere fiber, which is therefore very hard to come by, and expensive when a source is found. The soft spinnable fleece is worth the trouble though, for it makes the most delicate of sweaters or scarves.

Finishing off a weaving of mohair and alpaca homespun, which is shown in color on page 72.

The long hair of the *alpaca* is clipped or sheared every year, a large animal yielding as much as seven pounds of fleece. The fibers are straighter and finer than sheep's wool, and can be from eight to 24 inches long. Many beautiful ponchos are made from them by knitting or weaving the long silky hair, which can be spun carded or uncarded. Try combining on your own cards alpaca and the soft hair of a pet cat, or opposum from a fiber dealer, in addition to the more usual blends of alpaca and wool.

The two small wild members of the family still roam the cold high peaks. The reddish-tinged fibers of the *vicuña*, which range from yellow through brown shades, are the finest of any wool-bearing animal — even cashmere runs a poor second. The inner hairs are used, and they are only two one-thousandths of an inch thick. You can see why the Incas used to hunt this animal only for royalty, and why it costs a king's ransom, even today, to wear a coat woven of this finest of all yarns.

Fibers from the Farm

Do you live near a farm, a riding stable, a dairy, or a breeding ranch for one of the rare North American animals — the buffalo of our western plains (bison) or the far north's musk ox? Each of these large shaggy animals, as well as horses and cows, sheds or needs to be trimmed in the spring, and if you inquire in advance, perhaps the local rancher or zookeeper will collect some of the fibers for you.

Horsehair has been woven into fabrics for many uses, but is very rough. Unless you are atoning for your sins, don't wear it next to your body. Rugs, wall hangings, and purses can be made from the long hairs of tail and mane. I get these each spring when my daughter trims her horse's mane. In Sweden, beautiful yarns are spun of a mixture of *cowhair* and wool.

Like the camel, the buffalo has very soft under hair. In addition to spun *buffalo hair,* the Indians used whole buffalo hides as well. An arctic musk ox is very hard to encounter, but I hope that as the northern Indians and Eskimos succeed in increasing the herds, which they now use to knit delicate *quiviut,* or *musk-ox hair* shawls, we shall be able to obtain it.

Even our wild friends supply fur that can be combined with wool or other fibers to make conversation-piece yarns. If you don't have pet raccoons as we did, then *raccoon, opossum,* or even *mink hair* can be obtained from fiber dealers. Look at the fiber content of the next pair of "wooly" gloves you buy — raccoon is sometimes used commercially with synthetics to make a very light, warm blend.

One word of caution: don't try to gather fiber from any animal unless you know from personal experience that it is tame. No matter how friendly they look, wild animals and farm animals can sometimes be dangerous. Buffalo and musk oxen have bad manners — they charge without warning; the patient-looking camel has the nastiest habit of biting and spitting at people that bother him; and even a cow might turn out to be a bull, and decide to collect some fiber from *you*!

Silk

Even kings and queens, emperors and empresses have been eager to adorn themselves with the produce of the lowly silkworm. Worm! Sometimes the word evokes unpleasant thoughts. This one, however, is really a caterpillar — the larva of a moth that eats mulberry leaves and spins a delicate cocoon. The Chinese tale about the discovery of silk is that a princess dropped one of these cocoons into her teacup by accident, and saw that it unravelled into a long shimmering fiber. Whether the story is accurate of not, it bears much truth. The silkworm was domesticated three thousand or more years ago in China, and one of the important procedures in turning the cocoons into silk is immersing them in very hot water (not tea, at least nowadays) to remove the natural gum, or "sericin," that holds them together.

The secrets of silk culture were well guarded by the Chinese until, in 552, two monks smuggled some of the precious silkworm eggs to Constantinople in hollowed-out bamboo walking sticks. From there, silk culture and manufacturing spread around the world. Today, Japan, China, India, and France produce most of the raw silk, but the United States joins them in being a major silk processor. Many mulberry trees were planted in America during the 17th and 18th centuries in a zealous effort to start a native silk industry. However, the need for much cheap manual labor has always prevented the industry from taking hold.

The cocoons are steamed or soaked in hot soapy water, and then unreeled after the gum dissolves. Actually each fiber is a double filament of silk — about 3,000 feet long — and the spider-web thin strand is so delicate that it must be immediately combined with other fibers to produce a strong continuous thread thick enough to handle. From three to 12 of the double filaments are twisted and reeled up together on spools. This is called raw silk. The reeled, twisted fibers are then twisted together again with a number of other fibers of raw silk in a process called "throwing," to produce the desired weight and texture of

Openwork tapestry weaving by students. The warp is of handspun linen; the filling is of handspun Haitian cotton and nature-dyed shades of green (ragweed, lamb's quarters, goldenrod), rose-brown and black (logwood bark), orange (onion skins), and yellow (forsythia).

Knit and woven pillows by students. Pillows at left and middle are natural sheep and goat colors, woven on four-harness table loom. The colored pillow is knit from onion-dyed wool in shades of rust (chrome), yellow, orange, and lime green from carrot tops.

Scarf woven of alpaca and mohair. The mohair, which is used for the warp and filling, is commercially dyed and spun. The alpaca, which shows as the darker shades in the filling, is handspun and undyed.

Horse's parade saddle blanket, woven by author with assistance of students, on four-harness table loom. The Rya fringing of undyed yarn is made by pulling out filling into loops, knotting, and then cutting the loops. The rose color is logwood dyed, the tan is from inner bark of white birch, and the brown is from hulls of black walnuts.

A hanging of many colors and textures done by students on a four-harness table loom, with handspun Haitian cotton and Greek goat yarn.

yarn. Although throwing is a twisting process, it is essentially different from spinning, because it is a twisting of fibers that are already *long* enough to be yarn. Spun silk, on the other hand, is waste silk from the ends of a cocoon, broken cocoons, or short fibers, spun up just like wool. I never comb or card silk. It is too delicate, and can be spun as it is.

Silk for handspinning can be purchased in various forms. If in cocoon form, silk clinging to the cocoons can be spun from the hand, and the cocoon can be chopped up and carded to make more spinnable strands and nubs to combine with wool. If in long tops, which have been combed, separate lengthwise into slivers and spin as with wool. "Hankie" is the more processed, reeled silk that has been packaged into a layered square. Hankies are opened or "fumphed" by taking gentle short pulls at diagonal corners until one long strand results. I invented the word "fumphing," for that is the sound made by the silk as it is pulled on. Bulk silk, the waste from silk manufacture, is a fluffy mass that can be treated as any other fiber bundle containing various lengths.

"Fumphing" a "hankie" of silk to get a long strand for spinning from the packaged, reeled fibers. In commercial processes, reeled silk is "thrown", not spun, to create thread strong enough to use.

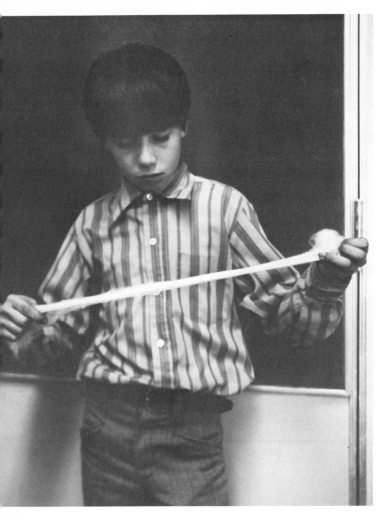

The long strand almost ready for spinning.

Not all of the gum has been removed in the original washing of the cocoons, and some of it helps to hold the separate strands together during the reeling and throwing processes. Therefore, silk is often woven before being completely degummed and dyed. If you are planning to dye your handspun silk yarn, you should wash it, too. Silk dyes brilliantly, and generally does not need the high temperatures in the dyebath that wool does. However, soaking times, mordants, and amount of plant material needed may vary.

An interesting project would be the raising of silkworms. Although you don't have to smuggle the eggs out of China anymore, they can be difficult to obtain. Try any large biological supply house you know of, or see the list of suppliers at the end of the book. About one ounce of silkworm eggs yields one hundred pounds of cocoons, and roughly nine pounds of silk. However, you would need a forest of mulberry trees to feed all the silkworms! Plan your experiment for only a few eggs.

The pinhead size eggs of the silkworm (*Bombyx mora*) are kept indoors over the winter, and hatch in the spring, when the mulberry *(Morus alba)* puts out its leaves. The larva are kept at 72 degrees F. in stacked open drawers covered with perforated paper on which first chopped, and later whole, leaves are placed. The leaves must be very fresh and replaced every day. In about six weeks, the worms have shed their skins four times, and have grown to about three inches. This is ten thousand times the size they were before! Now they are ready to spin their cocoons, on convenient cones of cardboard that you provide when they begin to raise their heads up "looking" for a place to begin spinning. It takes them from three to five days to complete the cocoon. If left undisturbed, the caterpillars would mature inside and emerge as moths in a little over two weeks. However, they puncture the cocoons to get out, which breaks the long filament in a number of places. Therefore the cocoons are left in the sun or otherwise dried and heated to stop the natural process.

Silk is also made by other silkworms. One of the wild silks, which are called "tussah" silk, comes from a Chinese silkworm that lives on oak leaves. Even moths in America that eat ailanthus or osage-orange leaves have produced silk, however the quality of all of these wild silks is inferior to that produced by the little mulberry silkworm, which has lived with man for so long that it cannot live in the wild anymore.

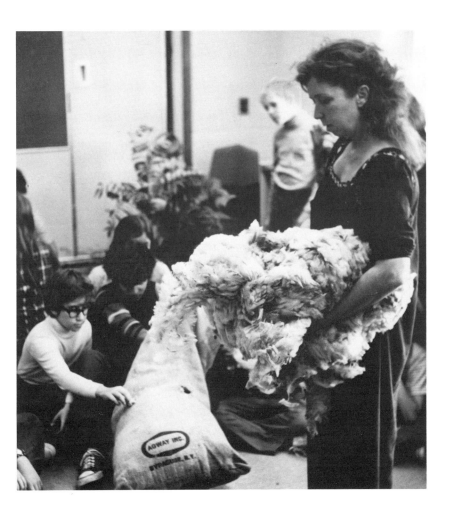

6 Making Use of Homespun

But what do you do with it? I am asked that question so often about yarn made on the spindle or spinning wheel. Most people find it a bit difficult to accept the fact that yarn made by hand can be put to any practical use. The answer is simple: *we do what was done with it centuries ago, and is still being done wherever people knit, crochet, stitch, hook rugs, and weave.*

Most women — and nowadays even some men — can do a little knit and purl, can crochet a potholder or two, and have experimented, even if only when children, with a sampler of needlepoint stitches. There are many hand-craft instructions available (see the Bibliography) so there is no need to go into detail here. Instead, most of this chapter will be on weaving, an ancient and satisfying craft that many people feel reluctant to try their hands at. Perhaps they feel it is too difficult, or too much equipment is needed. If you feel this way, just flip through the pictures here. My young students have very happily adapted to weaving, even on a four-harness loom, and have had a great deal of fun learning how.

Knitting, Crochet, Stitchery, Needlepoint, Rug Hooking

These crafts have appealed to people for centuries, perhaps as ways to create fabrics from the bulky yarns that could not be easily woven, or to create lacy edgings and decorative borders on already woven cloth and household fabrics. Even when it was no longer necessary to make fabrics by hand, people continued to enjoy the textile crafts as creative ways to make useful or purely decorative pieces.

TOOLS AND MATERIALS

The equipment for these crafts is minimal: a pair of knitting needles and several sizes of crochet hooks, including some large metal or plastic ones, several sizes of crewel or tapestry needles and a background fabric for needlepoint, sharps and an embroidery hoop for stitchery, and a latchet hook and rug canvas for rug hooking.

The most important element is the homespun yarn. Either natural or dyed, it stands so well on its own merits that complicated stitches are unnecessary, and even the simplest design brings out the unique character of the material. The handspinner has even more freedom of choice than the craftsman who buys yarn — thick or thin yarns can be spun to order, slub yarns can be created for variety, blends can be made on the cards, and plied yarns for extra strength or varied color combinations can be created on the spinning wheel.

Large knitting needles work well with bulky homespun, allowing the texture of the yarn to show clearly in simple stitches.

An embroidery hoop, sharp needles, background fabric, and nature-dyed yarns are all you need to make very colorful crewel or embroidery samplers.

Do you want a thin yarn for delicate crochet and knitting? Try spinning line flax, or a blend of cotton and linen sometimes called cot-lin. An expert spinster will be able to spin a yarn as thin as sewing thread out of wool alone! You can spin a single strand of wool about the thickness of

Crochet is a good technique for homespun, and the simple stitches done in single-ply yarn are very easy to learn.

When using homespun, the yarn itself is the most important element. The student is rolling a ball of yarn from a skein before beginning her project.

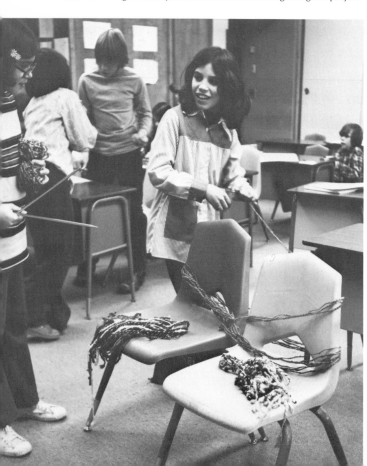

four-ply knitting worsted out of the fine, straight wool of the extra diamond or diamond section of a fleece. Knitting and crochet are easier for beginners with a single-ply yarn, because there is less tendency for the needle to split or fray the strand. Alpaca, a fiber that is straighter than wool, and of longer staple than most wool fibers, is also an excellent choice for these fine yarns.

Do you want a rya-type wool for rug hooking? It is usually imported from Scandanavia, and therefore hard to find in our yarn stores, but you can spin a thick single ply from the prime or britch section of a fleece that will suit the purpose very well. Some rya wools are two ply, and you can use the same type of fleece to spin and then ply two thin strands together.

To approximate a Persian type of yarn, used in tapestry and crewel embroidery, ply together two single thin-spun strands of a fine but curly fleece. And think of the subtle shades you can use in your stitchery or bargello work when you have personally dyed the yarns the natural way, controlling each dyelot to the exact deepness of color you require.

Stitchery of many types can be done with homespun: For crewel embroidery, bargello, and tapestry, all the equipment necessary is some needlepoint canvas, or plain-weave cloth, and large-eyed needles. Designs for homespun stitchery should be kept simple to show yarn to advantage.

TECHNIQUES

The handspinner's needlecraft techniques do not really vary from the traditional ones. Except for winding your ball of yarn from the spindle or spool on the wheel instead of from a packaged skein, and for using only simple knit and purl and basic single, double, and triple crochet stitches to show off the natural variations in the yarn, you will be able to apply everything you already know about crafts to the beautiful colors and textures of homespun. Easy techniques and available, small equipment make projects with homespun very suitable for group work. Each craftsman can choose the technique he or she already knows, or learn a new one in a very short time. Most important, everyone can be doing a different thing, and there will always be enough material to go around.

Large projects can be worked on by more than one person. For instance, small squares of knitting or rounds of crochet done by many different people can be joined together to form lap robes. A rug can be hooked by one person one day and another the next, with no loss of artistic effect, once the initial design and colors are decided on. To get started on a rug-hooking project, cut four-inch strands of homespun to create a deep pile. With a magic marker, draw a simple design on a rug canvas with four to six holes to the inch. Then using the latchet hook, work in one strand of thick-spun or two strands of thin-spun yarn for each stitch. In weaving, as you will see, a whole class can participate by taking turns at the loom.

A rug-hooking project, showing design drawn on rug canvas with felt-tipped pen, and pile made from previously cut four-inch strands of homespun.

The technique is very simple: insert latchet hook . . .

. . . and draw through a loop of the doubled yarn, making a knot.

Weaving

Weaving is the second oldest craft known to man — that is, if you ask a spinner. A weaver would say that weaving is even older than spinning, having been practiced with unspun materials such as grasses and reeds used in woven basketry. From its simple beginnings, weaving has evolved in many directions, producing tapestries fit for a castle wall, as well as the humblest plain-weave toweling. Its techniques and equipment have become more and more complex, too, and you will find it easier to learn about them while doing various types of weaving yourself.

FINGER WEAVING

What is it that makes a *woven* piece of cloth? Two sets of threads, one vertical, called the warp, and one horizontal, called the filling, or weft. The vertical threads are held taut by a loom, and then the horizontal threads, which in practice usually consist of a long single thread that weaves back and forth, are interlaced between them, with the aid of a shuttle. As man first spun with his fingers, so too did these fingers serve as his first loom and shuttle.

In class one day we finger-wove sashes with thick homespun. Five long strands of one color were alternated with four long strands of another color to form the warp, which was made as long as required to circle the waist and hang free on both ends, as well as an additional 12 inches for the amount of shortening, called "take-up" that would occur as the filling was woven in and out. Our loom, which held the nine warp threads tight, was a hook, table leg, or chair at one end, and the weaver's hands at the other end. The filling thread was a longer piece of homespun of a third color, at least twice as long as the warp, and the shuttle, which helps the filling thread go over and under the warp threads, was the weaver's fingers.

There are two ways to get the filling thread over and under the warp. The simplest to explain (but the hardest to do) is to pick up every other warp thread and push the filling under it. When you are finished with the row, turn the filling around and retrace its steps, but wherever you passed the filling *under* a warp thread before, pass it *over* on the return.

The other way is to pick up all the proper threads at one time, creating a group of upper threads and a group of lower threads. The space in between them is called the "shed," and it is very easy to pass the filling thread through it, forming the first row. Then reverse the shed: make all the upper threads lower threads, and all the lower threads upper threads, and pass the filling back through to form the second row. That's all there is to it.

Finger weaving. The table leg is one end of the loom and the weaver's hand is the other. Filling, shown in his right hand, is woven back and forth without a shuttle.

Creating a shed with the weaver's fingers. First the odd number of warp threads is raised and the even number lowered.

Let's see how it works. After tying all the warp threads plus the one long filling thread to the chair or table leg, we arranged them into upper and lower groups, forming the shed, by picking up the odd number of ends — the five strands of one color — first. We raised them with our fingers, and passed the filling through. Next, we lowered the odd number of ends, and raised the even number — the four strands of the other color — creating a second shed. By repeating this process, we wove a solid band, and when it was finished, made a knot at the end to secure the sash. Unwoven yarn from the warp ends was made into a fringe, beaded, or elaborated with macramé.

After passing the filling through, the shed is reversed by lowering the odd number of threads and raising the even number.

The process is repeated to weave a solid band.

Unwoven warp yarn forms the fringe at the end of the sash.

TAPESTRY WEAVING

There are reasons for weaving the hard way, picking up each warp thread by hand rather than creating a shed from a large number of warp threads at once. Instead of pushing the filling through the shed in one long sweep, the weaver can direct it carefully over, under, around, and even backwards through a variable number of warp threads, and he can stop one color of filling and start another in midstream. The weft is carried along by the fingers or in some cases by small wooden bobbins.

The one thing the weaver can't do with his hands, because they are occupied in creating intricate patterns to cover the warp, is to hold the warp threads taut. From the earliest start of weaving on his fingers, man began to employ what nature provided, in the forms of trees and branches, as his looms. He first attached his warp only at one end, by looping it over a long horizontal tree branch. He kept the free ends of the warp threads under tension by weighting them with stones, wove his filling in and out, and then cut the warp free of the branch when he was ready to use the cloth.

No sheds are created in this tapestry weaving on a rigid frame. Instead, the weaver carries the filling under and over the warp threads he chooses, with the aid of a needle that serves as a shuttle. Note that there are several colors of filling on needles which are being woven at the same time.

Branch Weaving.

The warp and weft don't have to be made of the same yarn. In the patterned weaves usually called tapestry weaves, the warp doesn't show at all, and therefore does not need to be dyed, or to serve any decorative purpose. In using homespun yarn for weaving, be sure to choose a strong yarn for the warp, although you can use the most fragile, delicately spun yarn for the filling without weakening the structure of the whole piece. In some decorative pieces much warp shows, and is therefore a part of the design. For such an "openwork" weave, choose your warp thread not only for strength but to blend with or enhance the filling.

Try creating a hanging, openwork or weft-faced, from a branch loom. Find a pliable but firm branch, such as one from a grape or other vine, and bend it into the shape you want. Then lash the ends together securely, and wrap the warp around the outer edges. The warp can be in a fixed vertical pattern or in a more random one, depending on the final effect you want. Weave a row or two of *warp yarn used as filling,* at the outer edges. This secures the warp to the branch. Now begin weaving with the fillings you have chosen, and don't worry about removing the hanging when it is finished, because the branch serves as a frame.

A different kind of branch weaving, suspended on a dowel. The branch will serve as a convenient hanger for the piece when the weaving is finished.

A free-form branch weaving in progress. After the warp has been wrapped around a bent branch, a row of warp used as filling is woven in to help secure the warp to the branch.

Picture Frame or Board Loom.

Tapestry weaving can be done on a simple loom made from an old picture frame or artist's canvas stretcher. Drive a row of nails, at the same intervals, along the top and bottom of the frame, and wrap your warp on these, first around a top nail, then a bottom nail, and so on. When finished weaving, merely detach the warp from the nails, with the aid of a crochet hook.

An even simpler method would be to wrap the warp completely around the frame, or even around and around a solid board. This produces a warp that can be woven on both sides of the frame or board, so that the piece will be twice as long as the loom when finished. The warp must be cut at one end to remove it from the board.

A larger loom of the same sort.

A picture-frame type of loom can be warped on nails placed carefully at regular intervals along the top and bottom of the loom.

A solid board can also be used as a loom by wrapping the warp entirely around it. If woven on both sides and cut at one end, the weaving will open up into a piece twice as long as the board.

LOOMS WITH SHED HOLDERS

From ancient times, weavers have created systems for raising and lowering part of the warp to create sheds. In the finger weaving experiment you saw how every other thread (all of one color, in this case) was lifted, while the alternate threads were lowered. This produces a tabby, or plain, weave, which is often graphically described as "one over, one under." Sheds are made to produce many different weaves: raising every two threads produces a basket weave, "two over, two under," or just raising those threads necessary to create a motif produces a tapestry, or jacquard, weave. From simple principles, weavers create an almost endless variety of ways to weave the warp and filling together.

Navajo Looms.

The beautiful rugs of the Navajo Indians were and still are woven on looms made of lashed together tree trunks and boughs (see picture on page 76), and with a "heading" of warp used as filling, to secure the warp threads temporarily to the loom, somewhat as you did with the branch weaving. The weaver sits on the ground in front of his upright frame loom. Inside the frame are suspended two dowels, called "warp beams," around which the warp has been wound. The bottom beam is attached directly to the frame by ropes, but the top beam is first attached to another dowel or branch, which is tied by a rope pulley to the top of the frame, and serves to adjust the tension on the warp.

In class, we have used this set-up for working the filling in and out with the weaver's fingers. However, the Navajos open sheds, in the patterns they want, with two willow branches and a flat piece of wood of about the same length as the branches. They attach strings, called "heddles," to the set of warp threads that will be lifted for one shed. Then the willow branches, called "shed rods," are hooked and placed on the strings so that moving the rods apart physically raises and lowers the shed. There are two positions for the shed rods: one, in which they are apart, is called the "pull shed," because it pulls on the heddles, and the other, in which they are together, is called the "stick shed," because the flat shed stick is inserted and turned on its end, creating enough space for the filling thread to go through.

With or without sheds, the filling must be pushed down tight after every row. This process is called "beating," and ensures that as little warp as possible will show through the finished weaving. Beating is done by the Navajos with a weaving fork of polished wood, which looks like a salad fork. You can use a table fork or even a strong comb for the same purpose.

When the Navajo weaver had woven so much that he couldn't reach the next row, he would loosen the tension ropes, bringing the whole piece down, sew the already woven part tightly to itself at the bottom, and begin weaving again.

A Navajo beater being used to push down the filling. Note how the design for this tapestry weaving has been "drawn" in with dark thread.

A kitchen fork also serves well as a beater.

Backstrap, waist, and lap looms.

Can you imagine sitting inside a horizontal loom, so that your back creates the tension on the warp? A backstrap, or waist, loom is of a kind still in use today, especially in South America, where it has been used for centuries. Some of the beautiful and complex ancient Peruvian textiles, which can be seen in museums today, were made on such looms. The principles are the same as before, but there is no rigid frame. Instead, the warp is wrapped around two dowels or sticks, and the dowel closest to the weaver is connected to a strap or sash that goes around the weaver's waist. While weaving, you press back on the backstrap to keep tension on the warp, which can only be woven with filling within the arm-reach of the weaver. Once this stage has been reached, the weaving thus far completed can be rolled up by the use of the dowel closest to the weaver and more weaving can commence.

Warping a backstrap, or waist, loom on a dowel.

Weaving on the backstrap loom. A warped dowel is attached to a convenient hook. Next, the rigid heddle is threaded, and the other end of the warp attached to the near dowel. Finally the weaver gets "inside" the loom by running a comfortable sash around her waist to keep tension on the warp, and begins weaving the large shuttle through a shed that will be created by the heddle.

An interesting feature of most of these looms is the rigid heddle. Although some have string heddles, as in the Navajo loom, the function of making sheds and beating down the filling can be combined in a single implement, looking like a comb that has been closed off on both top and bottom. The "teeth" of this rigid heddle have holes in them through which the warp for one shed goes; the warp for the other shed slides between the teeth. You can see why this system is often called the "hole-and-slot heddle." When the heddle is raised, it pulls up the warp that is threaded through the holes, creating one shed. When it is lowered, it drops the same warp below the other warp threads, creating the second shed. In between, the filling is passed through, and the heddle is drawn forward forcibly, to become a very effective beater.

The same type of heddle is used in the slightly more intricate "lap loom," which is like a rigid-frame variation of a horizontal backstrap loom, except that no backstrap is needed because the frame itself keeps tension on the warp. The lap loom features a rigid heddle and a revolving warp and cloth beam. These are like the dowels at the two ends of the backstrap loom already described, on which the warp is wrapped. In a revolving-beam loom, pieces much longer than the size of the loom can be woven. As the showing warp is completed, more warp is rolled off the beam farthest away from the weaver (warp beam) and the woven portion is rolled up and out of the way on the other beam (cloth beam). This continuous warp system enables you to weave up to three yards of cloth, in widths up to 24 inches. A loom of this type introduces applying the warp properly in preparation for weaving — "dressing" or "warping up" — and taking it off properly, as done on the large looms we will next describe.

The hole-and-slot heddle on a lap loom. When raised, the heddle creates the first shed; when lowered, it pulls the warp threaded through the holes *below* the sliding warp in the slots, creating the second shed. A revolving warp beam can also be seen here.

FOUR-HARNESS TABLE LOOM

Just as I feel that spinning is for everyone, so too I believe that with patience on the part of the teacher, and eagerness to learn in the student, weaving is also for everyone. It was a challenge to teach fifth graders, students of eleven to twelve years old, how to use the four-harness table loom, but they learned. And if they did, you can too!

This loom allows the weaver to employ a great variety of patterns in his work by using the same basic elements as less complex looms: rigid frame, heddles for making sheds, a rigid comb, called a "reed," for a beater, and a revolving warp and cloth beam. Many professional weavers use the loom or a larger floor version of it. I will touch here only on the fundamentals in preparing and weaving on this loom, as entire books have been written on just this one subject. If you have the opportunity to work on a four-harness table loom, you will undoubtedly want to read further, but the following brief introduction should help you put its equipment into perspective. No matter how complex it looks, it was all developed to make weaving easier — there is nothing you can do on this loom that couldn't in principle be done by finger weaving. If you are a weaver already, perhaps this will encourage you to teach the principles, which are based on what the student knows from simpler looms, plus the idea of a harness, to beginners.

The Harness.

You know what a harness is when it is on a horse; sometimes it links a pair of horses together, to coordinate their efforts. The four harnesses on a loom are like a team of four horses pulling the warp threads. Each harness creates a different shed, and by using each of the four harnesses in different sequences, various woven patterns can be created very easily.

Each harness on the loom works like a separate system of string heddles, although the connections are made of wire not string. The warp is threaded through the heddles. The harness is a frame across which is connected a top and bottom bar that runs the width of the warp. To these are attached the wire heddles through which run individual warp threads. The harness is also connected to a lever on the loom that will raise the harness, thus pulling on the warp threads connected to it.

There are two basic ways in which a weaver makes his patterns or "drafts," on this loom. Just learning how they are created is a study in itself. To establish the pattern of a weave, you must both thread each harness in its own way

and raise the harness alone or in combination with other harnesses. Let's say you have threaded the first harness with every other warp thread, and the second harness with the alternate threads. If you then lifted both harnesses 1 and 2, you would not have any shed at all, because every thread would be up. But by raising either 1 or 2, a shed would be created through which to pass your filling. In addition, if you had threaded harness 3 with the alternate threads on harness 2, by raising harness 1 and 3 you would again create a shed. Harness 4 is also put to use in a like manner. How the harnesses are threaded initially depends on the pattern you wish to achieve. Once you have learned to thread, or dress, the loom properly for the different patterns, the harnesses can be lifted in various sequences to produce the weave, for example, by raising harnesses 1 and 3 for the first shed and 3 and 4 for the second.

It looks complicated doesn't it? Four harnesses of an eight-harness loom are going to be used. Later pictures show a single four-harness loom.

93

Preparing the Warp.

Before weaving, a warp of as many threads, or "ends," as required must be prepared. These will eventually be attached to the beams on the loom before and after they go through the reed and heddles. A reed is like a rigid heddle with no holes, only slots. It is mounted in the loom in such a way that it can be pushed forward after each pass of the shuttle, to beat down the warp. It is easiest for a beginner to prepare his warp ends equal to the number of slots, or "dents" in the reed. Half as many ends are required if every other opening is skipped; likewise, twice as many ends can be employed by threading two ends through every dent.

Instead of attaching each thread in a separate operation, the warp can be conveniently prepared on a warping frame. Basically, this is a frame or board with pegs around the perimeter on which the warp is wrapped. Later on, when cut at both ends of the circuit, the warp will open up so that it can be threaded through the loom. You can imagine what a tangle so many long threads could become if proper care is not taken to make sure they stay in order. To do this, the threads are crossed between the second and third peg of the frame in what is called the cross, to keep the warp from tangling hopelessly during the transfer to the loom.

First, the selected yarn is wound and counted on the frame. Remember that each completed circuit will open up into two warp threads or "ends" once on the loom. When the proper number of ends are on the frame, crossing as they should, the warp is then secured at the cross by inserting a strong piece of yarn and tying it in a loose loop with a double knot. Before removing the warp from the frame, it must be secured further by tying the ends together tightly in three or four places. A tied loop secures the cross. The next step is removing the warp from the last peg. The hand is inserted in the resulting loop, and the remainder of the warp is then "chained off" the warp frame, as one would do a chain stitch in crochet. In this case, however, the hand substitutes for the crochet hook, and all the warp threads together substitute for the single strand of the crochet yarn.

Now two lease sticks are inserted on either side of the cross. They are tied together at each end, through holes provided for this purpose, to prevent the threads of the cross from slipping out. A strong piece of yarn or string is passed through the holes and tied so that the lease sticks remain about an inch apart. Then, when the warp is taken to the loom, the lease sticks are taped to the front beam so they lie horizontally along it. One loop remains above the

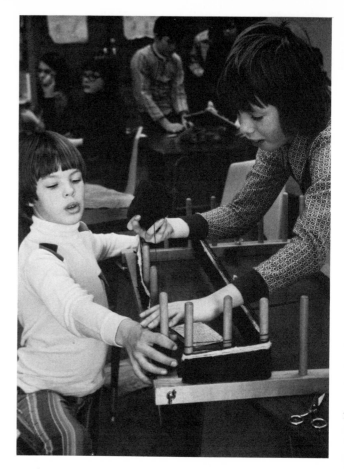

Working on a warping frame. Note the cross of the threads between the second and third pegs, which can be seen under ball of yarn.

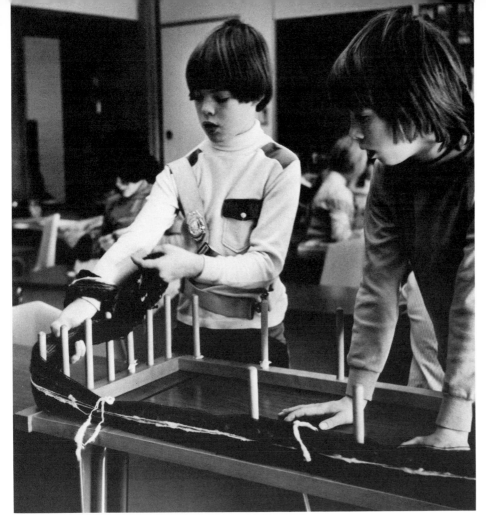

Next, the warp must be transferred, untangled, to the loom. To do this, the warp is chained off from the uncut end. Lease sticks will be placed at the cross of the warp, which can be seen at lower right.

Transferring the completed warp chain, with lease secured by two lease sticks.

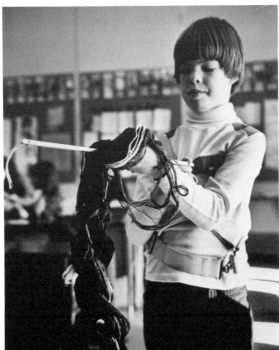

95

Sleying the reed with a reed hook. Many parts of the table loom can be seen clearly here: at right student leans over warp beam; hook is pointing to reed; harnesses with heddles pushed to sides are in front of reed, and you can see how the harnesses are attached, just under the top of the frame, to levers that will lift and lower them. Handles to the opposite set of levers, which cannot be seen, are at the left of the frame.

lease sticks, and the remainder of the warp hangs below it, neatly chained. The loop of the warp above the lease sticks is now cut, and each end is put through a dent in the reed, a process called "sleying the reed." When all the dents are filled, the ends are threaded through the chosen wire heddles, with the aid of a reed hook, which looks like a flat, wood-handled crochet hook. Finally, the warp is tied to the warp beam (at rear), the lease sticks removed, and the warp rolled up onto it. Next, the end loop of the warp chain is cut, and the remaining length of warp ends are tied onto the cloth beam at front. Actually, the warp ends are tied to a part of the apron, not directly to the beam. The apron is a cloth piece generally stapled to the beams; the warp ends are tied to a metal or wood bar which runs through the apron hem.

Weaving.

After the preparation, weaving seems simple. Sheds are formed by pushing down the proper levers on the loom, thus raising the harnesses. After each pass of the shuttle, the reed is used as a beater. If the piece is to be loosely woven, the reed is pushed down on the filling gently; for a tight weave, it is pushed down firmly. By passing the weft through the first shed, and changing sheds, the filling is secured. The initial end piece of filling, of some two inches, can be tucked into the second shed, or left out, or woven in later on with a crochet hook. When one filling runs out, or a new color is required, a new end of filling is run through the shed, overlapping the old end. After being beaten down with the beater, the ends blend. Then you change sheds and continue weaving with the new filling.

To remove the woven piece after it is finished, ends must first be detached from the warp beam and secured. Then the piece is unrolled from the cloth beam, and its ends detached and secured. Before cutting any ends, consider how your finished piece will look — leave long ends for a long fringe, short ends for a short fringe, and if no fringe is wanted, leave only enough to weave the ends unobtrusively back into the finished piece with a crochet hook. After being cut, at least every two ends are tied together, which holds the weaving firmly in place. There are many ways to finish a woven piece in addition to fringing: a hem can be made where appropriate, or the ends can be secured by machine stitching across the width of the fabric if the piece will only be viewed from the front.

Part of the fun of using the four harness loom in a group situation is that weavers can take turns so easily, since the set-up will stay in perfect order unattended. The pattern of the weave, once the order of the sheds is known, can be continued by anyone.

A top view of the loom, with shuttle being passed through the shed. The harness lever handles can be seen clearly.

After each pass of the shuttle, the reed is used as a beater. This is the
starting position.

It is always gratifying to be complimented on an article made with your own hands. After reading this book, when a friend exclaims, "Do you mean to say you knit this yourself?", you can answer with pride," I knit it. I spun the yarn, and I dyed it with pokeberry juice!" And perhaps some of our more adventuresome readers might be able to add, "I sheared the sheep to get the wool, too." However far you go into spinning and dyeing the natural way, we hope you will have a fuller gratification and a justifiable pride in your handcrafts.

Beater in the second position, which presses down the filling. Note that the shed shown here has been created by raising harnesses 3 and 4, as you can see by the raised levers at the side.

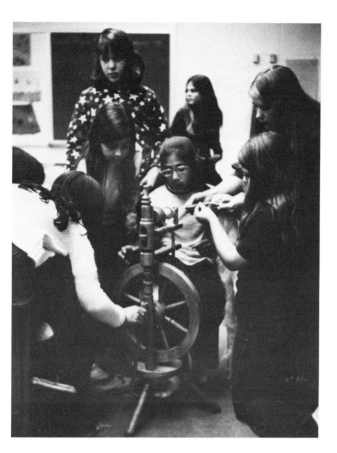

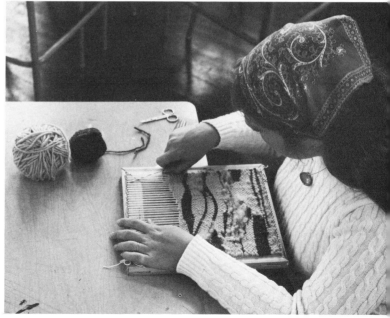

Sources of Supply

UNITED STATES

Christopher Farm, R.F.D. #2, Richmond, Maine 04357.
Yarn from their 350 Corriedale, Montdale, and Columbia sheep. Their yarn is mill-spun but nice.

City Chemical Company, 132 West 22 Street, New York, N.Y.
Mordants and other chemicals.

Clemes & Clemes, 665 San Pablo Avenue, Pinole, California.
Spinning wheels, supplies for spinning such as spindles, distaffs, cards, etc.

Earth Guild, Inc., 149 Putnam Avenue, Cambridge, Mass.
Dyestuffs, mordants, spinning wheels; and fibers (wool, alpaca, and various others).

Nilus LeClerc, Inc. L'Islet, Quebec, Canada.
Looms and a complete selection of weaving supplies.

R.A. Meisterheim, R.R. 6, Box 242, Dowagiac, Michigan.
Spinning wheels sold, repaired, and restored.

Natural Science Industries, Ltd., 51–17 Rockaway Beach Blvd., Far Rockaway. New York 11691.
"Silk Factory," kit for raising silk worms.

The Niddy-Noddy, Croton-on-Hudson, N.Y.
Unusual yarns, weaving, and spinning supplies.

Sargent-Welch Scientific Company, 7300 North Linder, Skokie, Illinois 60076. Biological supplies, including "Silk Garden" kit for raising silkworms.

Marguerite Shimmin, 2470 Queensberry Road, Pasadena, Calif.
Silkworm eggs. Write first for description of supplies.

Paula Simmons, Suquamish, Washington.
Handspun yarns and items woven of handspun yarn.

The Spinster, 34 Hamilton Avenue, Sloatsburg, N.Y. 10974.
Unique handspun yarns to order, fibers (Corriedale, Cheviot, Dorset, and Karakul fleeces, silk, alpaca, mohair, camel's hair, cashmere, cotton, flax).

Yarn Primitives, P.O. Box 1013, Weston, Connecticut 06880.
Imported handspun yarns, including alpaca, goat hair, cotton, and others.

CANADA

Handcraft House, 56 Esplanade, North Vancouver, British Columbia.

Village Weaver, 551 Church Street, Toronto, Ontario.

Mrs. E. Blackburn, R.R.#2, Caledon East, Ontario.

AUSTRALIA

Charles D. Bailey, 15 Dutton Street, New South Wales, Australia
Dyestuffs, fibers for spinning (fleece, cotton, silk, mohair).

UNITED KINGDOM

Spinning and weaving equipment:

Dryad, Northgates, Leicester.
Harris Looms, North Grove Road, Hawkhurst, Kent.
The Hand Loom Centre, 59 Crest View Drive, Petts Wood, Kent.
Arrol Young, Netherdale Galashiels, Scotland.
E.J. Arnold Ltd., Butterley Street, Leeds LS101AX.
Haldane & Co., Gateside, Fife KY14 7ST, Scotland

Fleece:

Dryad, Northgates, Leicester.
Ebenezer Prior Ltd., Dyson Street, Bradford, Yorkshire.
Haldane & Co., Gateside, Fife KY14 7ST, Scotland

Yarns:

Dryads, Northgates, Leicester.
Craftsman's Mark Ltd., Broadlands, Shortheath, Farnham, Surrey.
The Hand Loom Weavers, Fourways, Rockford, Ringwood, Hampshire.
Hugh Griffiths, Brookdale, Beckington, Bath, Somerset.
T.M. Hunter, Sutherland Wool Mills, Brora, Sutherland. (tweed yarns)
J. Hyslop Bathgate & Co., Victoria Works, Galashiels, Scotland.
Weavers Shop Ltd., Wilton Royal Carpet Factory, Wilton, Nr. Salisbury, Wilts. (6 ply and 2 ply rug wools and warp twine)

Bibliography

PLANT HANDBOOKS
Alvin and Kershaw. *The Observer Book of Lichens.* Warne, 1963.
Coon, Nelson. *Using Wayside Plants.* New York: Hearthside, 1957.
Craighead, John J., Frank C. Craighead, Jr., and Ray J. Davis. *A Field Guide to Rocky Mountain Wildflowers.* Boston: Houghton Mifflin, 1963.
Martin, W. Keble. *Concise British Flora in Colour.* Michael Joseph and Ebury Press, 1969.
McClintock and Fitter. *Pocket Guide to Wild Flowers.* Collins.
Peterson, Roger T. and Margaret McKenny. *A Field Guide to Wildflowers of Northeastern and North-central North America.* Boston: Houghton-Mifflin, 1968.
Stokoe (ed.) *The Observer Book of Wildflowers.* Warne, 1956.

NATURE DYEING
Adrosko, Rita J. *Natural Dyes and Home Dyeing.* New York: Dover, 1971.
Davenport, E. *Your Yarn Dyeing.* Sylvan Press.
Lesch, Alma. *Vegetable Dyeing: One Hundred and Fifty-One Recipes for Dyeing Yarns and Fabrics with Natural Materials.* New York. Watson-Guptill, 1970.
Robertson, Seonaid. *Dyes from Plants.* New York: Van Nostrand Reinhold, 1973.
Schetky, Ethel Jane, (ed.) "Dye Plants and Dyeing — A Handbook," from *Plants and Gardens,* Vol. 20, No. 3. New York: Brooklyn Botanic Gardens, 1964.
Thurston, V. *The Use of Vegetable Dyes.* Dryad.

SPINNING
Bowen, Godfrey. *Wool Away, The Art and Technique of Shearing.* New York: Van Nostrand Reinhold, 1974.
Channing, Marion L. *The Magic of Spinning.* Marion, Mass.: Channings, 1971.
Davenport, Elsie C. *Your Handspinning.* Pacific Grove, Calif.: Craft and Hobby, 1971; Sylvan Press.
Ellacott, S.E. *Spinning and Weaving.* Methuen.
Fannin, Allen. *Handspinning, Art and Technique.* New York: Van Nostrand Reinhold, 1971.
Kluger, Marilyn. *The Joy of Spinning.* New York: Simon & Schuster, 1971.
Morton, W.E. *An Introduction to the Study of Spinning.* Longmans Green.

WEAVING AND OTHER CRAFTS
Bennet, Noel and Tiana Bighorse. *Working with the Wool, How to Weave a Navajo Rug.* Flagstaff, Arizona: Northland, 1971.
Chetwynd, Hilary. *Simple Weaving.* Studio Vista.
Davenport, Elsie C. *Your Hand Weaving.* Sylvan Press.
Enthoven, Jacqueline. *The Stitches of Creative Embroidery.* New York: Van Nostrand Reinhold, 1964.
Hooper, L. *Hand Loom Weaving.* Pitman.
Kahlenberg, Mary Hunt and Anthony Berlant. *The Navajo Blanket.* Los Angeles: Los Angeles County Museum of Art (with Praeger).
Lind, Vibeke. *Practical Modern Crochet.* New York: Van Nostrand Reinhold, 1973.
MacKenzie, Clinton. *New Design in Crochet.* New York: Van Nostrand Reinhold, 1972.
Phillips, Mary Walker. *Creative Knitting.* New York: Van Nostrand Reinhold, 1971.
Rainey, Sarita R. *Weaving Without a Loom.* Oak Tree Press, 1969.
Regensteiner, Else. *The Art of Weaving.* New York: Van Nostrand Reinhold, 1970; Studio Vista.
Shillinglaw, Phyl. *Introducing Weaving.* Batsford, 1972.
Simpson, L.E. *The Weaver's Craft.* Dryad.
Walzer, Marilyn. *Handbook of Needlepoint Stitches.* New York: Van Nostrand Reinhold, 1971.
Wigg, Dora. *Let's Weave.* Evans Brothers, 1974.
Wildman, Emily. *Crochet.* Evans Brothers and Pan Books, 1974.
Wilson, Jean. *Weaving is for Anyone.* New York: Van Nostrand Reinhold, 1967.
Wilson, Jean. *Weaving is Fun.* New York: Van Nostrand Reinhold, 1972; Studio Vista.
Znamierowski, Nell. *Step-by-Step Weaving.* New York: Golden Press, Western Publishing, 1967; Evans Brothers and Pan Books, 1974.

PERIODICALS: UNITED STATES
Handweaver and Craftsman: 220 Fifth Avenue, New York, N.Y. 10001.
Shuttle, Spindle, and Dyepot: Handweaver's Guild of America, 1013 Farmington Avenue, West Hartford, Conn.

PERIODICALS: UNITED KINGDOM
Quarterly Journal of the Guild of Weavers, Spinners, and Dyers.
British Pure-bred Sheep; National Sheep Breeders' Association
Cotton Board, The Royal Exchange, Manchester 2.
International Wool Secretariat Publications, Dorland House 18–20 Regent Street, London, S.W.1.

Index

THE END

BY
PHYLLIS
MAKRIS

Very Good!
A